Time Management

Screw Self Discipline With This Uncommon Guide to Conquer Procrastination, Boost Productivity, and Get Organized

Time Management

Disclaimer Notice:

Please note the information contained within this document is for educational and entertainment purposes only. Every attempt has been made to provide accurate, up to date and reliable complete information. No warranties of any kind are expressed or implied. Readers acknowledge that the author is not engaging in the rendering of legal, financial, medical or professional advice.

By reading this document, the reader agrees that under no circumstances are we responsible for any losses, direct or indirect, which are incurred as a result of the use of information contained within this document, including, but not limited to, —errors, omissions, or inaccuracies.

Table of Contents

Bonus

Thanks for making it this far in your education. If you want the real multiplier effect and to take your business skills to the next level, I recommend the easy-to-follow quick tips below. Whether you are running a company or just trying to free up some time so you can spend more time doing the things you love, get more done this week or your money back ;) (it's free!).

Go to https://funnelb.leadpages.co/smarter-not-harder-business/

Top 10 Productivity Tips & Hacks GUARANTEED to Unlock Massive Amounts of Time, Crush Decision Fatigue, and Skyrocket Your Efficiency and Effectiveness

Link: https://funnelb.leadpages.co/smarter-not-harder-business/

Introduction

Time. If the whole universe was to be described in a word, it would not be space or matter or light or electrons or any of such quasi scientific terms. It will be time. Because indeed, it is time and time only that is the most efficient and accurate yardstick of what has happened, what is happening and what will happen.

In fact, the importance of time can never be highlighted enough. It is the only commodity that once lost, is lost forever. It can never be bought back, no matter how much you wish to or strive to. One of the earliest fantasies of mankind, and perhaps which still continues to be one, is the endeavor to regain lost time. Isn't it cruel irony that men have attempted and failed in this pursuit, time and again! As Benjamin Franklin rightly put it, "lost time will never be found again".

One of the most common traits, of successful people from all walks of life, be it scientists, world leaders, industry captains or entrepreneurs, is their exceptional time management skills. So it is apparent that a person, who knows how to manage his time well, will excel in whatever task he undertakes. Lost time equates to lost opportunities, low productivity and lack of organization.

Another important element of time management is not about finishing all the given tasks in the time allotted for it. It is all about doing a portion of the daily tasks that produce the maximum results. More about the application of the Pareto principle has been highlighted in the second chapter of this book!

No matter what you do in life or intend to do, the biggest hurdle to reaching the top is procrastination. It is like an evil drug that draws you into its tangles the more you exercise it. Seize the moment, act upon it and all your aims and objectives will be attained sooner than later. On the other hand, shirk away from your responsibility and procrastinate, and success will indeed prove to be that silver unicorn.

And this is the topic that this book intends to address. In here, you will find the various techniques for managing your time in the most efficient and exceptional manner possible. I will give you all you need to know about how proper management of time will end up boosting your productivity, as well that of those around you. Embrace the techniques given in here and realization of your goals is not far away.

I thank you for purchasing this book and hope that you find it useful, informative and above all, worth your time!

Chapter 1: Time Management and Its Importance

Often, we end up doing things in the last minute because of lack of proper planning of our time and procrastination. Procrastination can be our biggest enemy, especially when we cannot afford to lose time. We don't realize the importance of time till we are pressed for it. In this chapter, we shall look at what time management is and understand the importance of time management and how it benefits us.

What is Time Management?

Before we venture any further into this book, it is important for us to understand the concept of time management. Often, we wish that we had more than 24 hours in a day. We desire for more time to finish all the tasks. The simple truth is that it is entirely possible to finish all the stipulated tasks assigned to us within the stipulated time if we plan our time properly.

Time management is nothing but the way in which we organize and plan the time to be spent on each activity. We often fall short of time because we tend to spend more time on redundant activities, which will leave us with very less time for important activities. Hence, when you learn to plan ahead and allot a specific time for each task, you are actually managing your time. The purpose of time management is not just to save your time but also to increase your efficiency and productivity.

Though we tend to go by the myth that time cannot be managed, it is entirely possible to manage our time effectively with the aid of certain principles, tools and tips (which are highlighted in the later part of this book). Time management encompasses the following aspects:

✓ Setting up of an environment, which is conducive and motivating to work.
✓ Setting of goals.
✓ Sorting out priorities.
✓ Taking efforts based on the priorities and which are goals-centric.
✓ Reduction in the time spent on tasks that do not fall under the priority category.
✓ Motivation to look forward to deadlines and handle them efficiently.

Hence, it is clear that time management is not a concept that can be understood and practiced in isolation.

Why Time Management Is Important

Managing your time is important for the following reasons:

✓ *Time is limited*

We all get the same amount of time in a given day. Time is a limited resource and it is not possible to regain lost time. So it is important that we use the limited time we have in a judicious fashion.

✓ *More accomplishments with less efforts*

We often find ourselves struggling to finish the things on our to-do list because we don't have the time to finish all those tasks. Even if we manage to somehow complete the tasks on time, we can never be sure of the quality of work. Hence, it is always lack of time or compromise in efficiency. Let us not neglect the amount of stress and efforts that go hand in hand when it comes to completing a plethora of things within a short span of time. Often, these could be those discouraging aspects for taking more initiative at work place.

On the other hand, when you manage your time well, you will realize that you will be able to accomplish more with less time and efforts instead of slogging. You will learn to increase your efficiency and productivity when you can manage your time better. This will in turn motivate you to take more initiative and responsibilities at work without killing yourself from exertion and stress.

✓ *Better decision making skills*
Seldom do we have the time to sit and analyze before we take important decisions. This is because we end up spending a considerable chunk of our time in accomplishing our goals and running behind missed deadlines. This should not be the case. It is important that we spend quality time in analyzing the pros and cons before we make any important decisions. This is important because the time spent on rectifying a hasty decision is much more than the time one ought to invest before making the decision.

When you manage your time properly, you will have sufficient time to weigh different options before making an important decision. You will also have time to go over the facts associated with each option in detail and understand them. This clarity can help you a long way in figuring out what you want. In other words, you will have enough time to take an informed decision. Informed decisions can add a lot of clarity and direction to our life.

✓ *Taking control of your life*

Most of the times, we are hazy about the details of the previous day. This is not because we are absent minded. This is because we spend our days running behind one deadline after another, flustered by the lack of time. So what we remember at the end of the day is the fact that we have accomplished the tasks within the deadline. Another aspect that needs to be taken into consideration is the fact that our lives are driven by our deadlines and the tasks that need to be finished. It is a deadline that determines how we spend the next few hours and not us. In other words, we have very less control over our lives and time. This can be quite a shocking epiphany when we sit and realize how our days are spent.

When you learn to manage your time, you are consciously aware of how you spend your time every day. You know how you want to spend every hour of your day and what meaning it holds for you. In other words, you learn to take control of your life. Your life stops being a wild goose chase the moment you learn to manage your time.

✓ *Learn more*

It doesn't matter if you are a student or working. If there is something that all of us have in common is that we are presented with opportunities to learn every day. But how many of us actually utilize these opportunities? We hardly have enough time in hand to go about our routine and meet all the deadlines for the day let alone have time to assess the different learning opportunities that we come across. This is such a shame if your job involves the component of on the job training.

You will realize that when you apportion time properly for everything , you will be able to finish the tasks on hand sooner than you think thereby giving you time to learn more about your job as well as new things. You will see yourself going places when you learn something on a daily basis. Not only does your knowledge improve but also your productivity does improve tremendously at this rate.

✓ *Say No to Stress*

Today, a major reason behind our increased stress levels is the fact that we struggle to finish the tasks assigned for the day. We end up getting flustered to finish everything on the list. You no longer have to run behind deadlines if you have a proper plan in hand. For instance, if you create a calendar for all the important deadlines, you will know beforehand how the month looks and you can plan accordingly instead of doing things in haste. You will find it relatively easier to handle deadlines if you have learnt the art of managing your time well.

✓ *Increased efficiency and productivity*

As mentioned earlier, when you learn to manage your time, you will realize that your efficiency is improved automatically. When your efficiency is increased, you will be able to get more work done in a limited span of time. In other words, your productivity is also increased. An important reason why our efficiency is affected is because we rush through the various things mentioned in our to-do list. The element of haste affects the accuracy of our work and in turn our efficiency. Similarly, we will not be able to pull off this tiring ordeal of chasing behind our deadlines. The exertion will certainly catch up and have an impact on our productivity in due course. Low productivity is associated with low levels of efficiency as well. Hence, it is important that we learn to manage your time well.

✓ *Self Discipline*

Time management instills a sense of discipline in us. How often have our friends given us the cold treatment for always bailing out on the social outings? How often have we missed out on important birthdays and anniversaries? And let us not forget the number of times we have forgotten to apply for something within the deadline.

When you have a set agenda for the day, there are only a handful of things that could go wrong. You learn to allocate time for everything, be it work or a phone call or some leisure activity. You end up disciplining your mind to work according to your time constraints. This way, you will find yourself having enough time for work as well as your leisure activities, without disappointing anyone. Apart from that, you will realize that your life is just not about work and will start realizing the importance of striking a balance between your work and social life.

These are some of the important reasons why you should manage your time. Time management is linked with all facets of your life and helps you apportion a time for every deserving task, without you missing out on anything.

✓ *Reducing Clutter*

Effective time management also helps create order in your life; it is a skill that can be used and one that can help you achieve long-term goals. The skill effectively creates a purpose in everything you do by helping you understand the whys of tasks you perform every day, and then helping you make positive strides to accomplish the small tasks that will build up to the goals what you have in mind.

Truth be told, some tasks are easier to stand or do when they have a purpose, for example; cleaning is not something that most of us like, but it is something that must be done if there is to be order and cleanliness in the home. This turns cleaning into a choice rather than a burden that we feel we must accomplish.

Being able to manage your time will ensure that the areas of your life that mean the most to you are allocated the most productive time and will thus tremendously contribute to your overall output. On the other hand, effective time management will help you work smarter rather than working harder. One of the most valuable resources available to you is time and once it is gone, you cannot get it back. Treating each task as a priority is a sure way to develop bad time management vices that eat into your time without adding an ounce of productivity. This "making every task an emergency" is very bad not only for our time but also for our wellbeing.

Chapter 2: Goal Setting

In the previous chapter, we had dealt with the importance of time management. An important aspect of time management is setting of goals. Having clear cut goals can help you channel your efforts as well as plan your time accordingly. In this chapter, let us look at the various aspects of goal setting in detail. The impact of goal setting when it comes to time management has been dealt in detail in the later chapters of this book.

Concept of Goal Setting

Goal setting is nothing but the formulation of a plan of action. Goals may be short term or long term. They can be specific as well as vague.

Goal setting has an impact on our outcomes. The four ways by which goal setting can affect our outcomes are as follows:

- ✓ **Choice**: Goals have the ability to narrow our attention. This in turn ensures that our efforts are made in the direction of the goals. In other words, we will not spend time on irrelevant or unnecessary activities.
- ✓ **Effort**: When we have set goals ahead of us, we tend to put in more efforts than required. When we have a certain target to achieve, we will not refrain from doing our job. In other words, we will not slacken our efforts. With increased efforts, it is

possible to achieve our goals within the stipulated time and with more efficiency. Goals also tend to energize us and help us to put in the requisite efforts to get the job done. This can be understood with a simple example where your goal is to cover a certain distance as a part of your daily walking routine. This will help you to walk till you reach the limit instead of giving up easily.

✓ **Persistence**: Most of us have the habit of giving up even at the slightest of distractions. One of the reasons for this lax attitude is the lack of definite goals to keep us motivated and on track. On the other hand, when you have a definite goal to achieve, you will figure out a way to achieve it against all odds. This is turn reflects on our persistence to do what it takes to achieve our goals.

✓ **Cognition**: Goals tend to have an impact on our behavior as well. For instance, when we have a specific goal to achieve within the stipulated time, we would do what it takes to achieve it. This reflects our gritty attitude as well as our penchant to finish things within the stipulated time. Sometimes, all you need is a proper and fulfilling goal to drop that lazy attitude and exhibit perseverance. This aspect of goal setting can be understood better with man's ability to develop strategies and tactics to tackle hurdles that he might face while trying to achieve his goals.

These four aspects of goal setting have a positive impact on the outcome. Goals help in keeping up the motivation levels of the person and in turn help them achieve it. High levels of motivation can work wonders in improving the morale of the individual and in turn his performance.

How to Set Goals

Now that we have seen the impact of goal setting on our performance, let us look at the steps to set goals.

✓ *Identify your long term goals:*
These long term goals are nothing but your life goals. For instance, it could be getting a certain degree or buying a house or getting the dream job. Take the time to understand what your long term goals are. This is very crucial, as this is the first step in goal setting.

✓ *Break the long term goals into smaller goals:*
Now that you have identified your long term goals, try breaking them into smaller goals. These smaller goals help you plan your day. In other words, these small goals form a part of your daily agenda. The importance of having an agenda is mentioned in detail in the later part of this book. To have a tab on them, write them down some place where you can see them. This will serve as a reminder of what you have to attain in order to achieve your life goals.

✓ *Alter your goals periodically:*
It is not necessary for the status quo to not change from the day you set the goals and today. As is normal, things are bound to change. It makes it important to alter our goals in line with the changes in order to make it feasible to achieve them. For instance, you can have a short term goal of running everyday for an hour at 6:00 a.m. in the morning because your long term goal is to stay fit. In case, the timing of your classes get shifted to 7:30 a.m. in the morning, it will not be possible for you to meet your

everyday goal of running. You will have to alter it accordingly and push it to another part of the day.

✓ *Make your goals specific:*

Ensure that your goals are specific. It is important that your goals are specific because they add a lot of focus to your efforts. When you have specific goals to achieve, you can achieve it easily within a short span of time. An example of a specific goal is your wish to buy a house in a certain suburban locality instead of just wishing to buy a house. When you pick out the locality as well, it makes it easier for you to be financially as well as mentally prepared for it.

✓ *Have goals that can be measured:*

Why do goals have to be measured? Well, simple; measuring goals makes it easier for you to evaluate your progress in terms of achieving them. For starters, if you wish to stay fit, you may have a short term goal of running at least five laps in the park near your home. In this case, your goal is to complete five laps and hence measurable. This way, you will be able to gauge your performance and the time taken to complete each goal.

✓ *Have realistic goals:*

Our goals should always be realistic, be it long term or short term. Having realistic goals is important because they have a direct impact on your motivation levels. For starters, if you have an unrealistic or an unattainable goal, no matter how hard you try, you will never be able to achieve it. This in turn will have an adverse impact on your motivation levels and your inclination to work. This will lead to deterioration in your performance levels as well. The amount of time wasted on this goal is another important disadvantage of having unrealistic goals.

On the other hand, when you have realistic goals, you will be able to achieve them with requisite amount of efforts and time. When you achieve your goals, you will be motivated to stretch your limits and have bigger goals. This can impact your performance and the quality of living in many ways. That's why it is important that you have achievable and practical goals, not just to boost your morale but also to save a lot of time and effort.

✓ *Track your progress:*

Your duty does not end with just setting goals. Unless we track our progress in achieving these said goals, we will not be able to assess the time spent on it. Going back to the previous example, we have a goal of running five laps a day in the nearby park. It is possible for you to complete the five laps within thirty minutes. However, if you run without a watch in hand, you may end up spending more than thirty minutes to complete the laps. This is why it is important to have measurable goals. But the purpose of having measurable goals is lost if you don't track your progress from time to time.

An effective way to track your progress would be to maintain a journal for this purpose. This way, you will be able to review your performance on a daily basis and identify any deviations. This will also help you identify unrealistic goals and help you take a decision accordingly. In other words, by keeping a regular track of your progress, it makes it possible for you to identify the time leaks and help you address that issue. You will be able to save a lot of time this way.

✓ *Never stop setting goals:*

As mentioned earlier, goals are an easy way to keep a check on your time as well as efforts. Hence, it is important that you keep challenging yourself from time to time. Never think it is alright for you to rest once you have accomplished a certain set of goals. Once you have accomplished a given set of goals, set new goals in line with your long term goals. This way, your time and efforts will be spent in a productive manner always. The idea here is not to transform you into robot that works hard all the time without having breaks. Even if you want to relax, you need to set that as a goal and allocate time for that particular activity. This will ensure that you don't have unallocated time because this is probably one of the ways you will end up doing something that will end up dragging for far too long. For instance, if you don't set a goal of sleeping from 9.00pm to 6.00am, you will probably find yourself not having any particular boundaries as far as what's done within this period is concerned. As such, you may end up watching a movie till midnight or waking up at 7.00am. Don't just set goals for those days when you want to use your time well; set goals all the time if you truly want to nurture the habit of following whatever it is you set yourself to do.

Now that you have seen the various aspects of goal setting, you will be in a better position to appreciate the importance of goals in time management when I talk about it in the later part of this book.

Chapter 3: Principles and Tools of Time Management

In this chapter, let us look at the various principles of time management. The Pareto principle of time management has been dealt in detail in the next chapter. These principles of time management makes it possible for us to channelize our time in an effective fashion. Let us look at them in detail.

ABC Analysis

ABC analysis is all about prioritizing our tasks for the day. The tasks for the day are prioritized based on the importance attached with them.

In a given day, our tasks to be accomplished can be categorized into one of the following types:

1. Type A: Important and urgent tasks
2. Type B: Important or urgent tasks
3. Type C: Neither important nor urgent tasks

Before you begin working, it is important that you classify the tasks for the day into one of the above three categories. Apply this principle towards the tasks for the month as well. Let us look at these types of tasks in detail now:

Type A:

The tasks that fall under this type possess the following features:

14

✓ These are highly important and urgent.

✓ They need to be done today.

✓ These are tasks that require your immediate action.

Hence, ensure that you complete these tasks without any unwarranted delay or without putting it off for another time.

Type B:

These tasks form a major part of your agenda. Most of these tasks will not have a specific deadline as in the case of type A tasks. However, it makes sense to allocate a suitable time for these tasks and get them done. The tasks falling under this category possess the following features:

✓ The task has a deadline, though not so rigid like Type A.

✓ A suitable time needs to be allocated for the completion of these tasks.

Type C:

The tasks falling under this category are not as important as tasks belonging to Type A or B. They may not be important or urgent. Nevertheless, it is necessary for you to complete them. Hence, once you have completed all the important tasks for the day, allocate the reminder time for these tasks.

Tasks to be discarded:

This ABC analysis helps you in not only identifying the tasks based on their priority but also identifying those tasks that need to be discarded. Tasks that ought to be discarded possess the following features:

✓ They are not important tasks.

✓ They are not urgent in nature.

✓ They are not necessary tasks.

Make sure that you do not waste time over these tasks.

Hence, ABC analysis helps you to allocate enough time for the priority tasks and ensure that they are completed without any undue delay.

The Eisenhower Method

The Eisenhower method makes it possible for you to identify those tasks that you should undertake and those you should discard. This method was discovered by the American General, Dwight D Eisenhower. He was entrusted with the responsibility of commanding 2 million soldiers during his tenure as a general. He created this technique in order to control the soldiers effectively.

According to this method, the tasks to be completed for the day were categorized into one of the four quadrants based on their urgency and importance. This method is built on the following famous quote of his:

"What is important is seldom urgent and what is urgent is seldom important".

Using the Eisenhower Method

Using this method is simple. Have your to-do list in hand. Ask yourself the following questions while going over the tasks – "Is it urgent?" & "Is it important?" Based on the answers, you can classify the tasks to be completed into one of the following quadrants:

✓ Quadrant One: Important and not urgent

✓ Quadrant Two: Important and urgent

✓ Quadrant Three: Not important and urgent

✓ Quadrant Four: Not important and not urgent

Let us go over these quadrants in detail now.

1. Quadrant One: Important and not urgent

Some examples of the tasks that fall under this category are as below:

✓ Building healthy relationships with your peers, neighbors etc.
✓ Physical exercises.
✓ Planning your day.

You should ideally be spending most of your time in this quadrant. The key to effective time management is to spend most of your time on the tasks that fall under this quadrant. However, most people tend to spend a lot of time on the other quadrants and seldom spend quality time for the tasks falling under this quadrant. If you realize that you are not spending enough time for this quadrant, ensure that you allocate some time in a day to focus on these important tasks.

2. Quadrant Two: Important and urgent

Some examples of the tasks that fall under this quadrant are as follows:

- Emergencies
- Deadlines
- Troubleshooting
- Serious urgent complaints
- Problem resolution, fire-fighting, fixes
- Staff issues or needs
- Reports and other submissions
- Meetings and appointments
- Project work with imminent deadline
- Significant demands from superiors or customers
- Planned tasks or project work now due
- Meetings and appointments

Since these tasks are important as well as urgent, these need to be attended to at once. In other words, they require your immediate attention. Another thing that has to be noted about the tasks that fall under this quadrant is that they are unwarranted and are often unplanned. Hence, there is no way by which we can foresee them and plan for these tasks.

Because of the urgency factor associated with it, we tend to spend a lot of time in this quadrant. Do not rest once you have completed the tasks that fall under this category. Ensure that you take proactive measures to minimize or eliminate the occurrence of these tasks again. For instance, you meet with an accident because you were riding a motorcycle without a helmet. This emergency can be easily avoided if you remember to wear the helmet the next time you take out your motorcycle.

3. Quadrant Three: Urgent and not important

The following are examples of tasks that fall under this category:

-   Incoming phone calls
-   Responding to emails
-   Colleagues who interrupt you in the middle of work
-   Irrelevant distractions
-   Unnecessary double-checking
-   Pointless routines or activities
-   Misunderstandings appearing as complaints
-   Ad-hoc interruptions
-   Trivial and 'off-loaded' requests from others
-   Dealing with accumulated unresolved trivia

As it is evident from the examples, these tasks are not highly important. However, it will not be possible for you to put off these tasks for a later time because of the urgency associated with them. For instance, it is not possible for you to completely ignore a colleague who is trying to get something clarified while you are in the middle of something important.

It is highly important that you find a way to deal with these tasks in the quickest manner possible. For instance, if you are working on an important task, you can put a 'Do not disturb' sign outside your room's door. This way, you can avoid the interruption of a colleague while working on something important. If some colleague manages to ignore the sign and come up to you, you can always politely say that you would be available to talk to them later. Identify similar ways to deal with these disturbances.

Ensure that you do not spend a lot of time in doing the tasks that fall under this category.

4. Quadrant Four: Not urgent and not important
Examples of the tasks that fall under this category are as follows:

- Time wasters such as Facebook and other social networking sites
- Procrastination
- Trivial work
- Aimless travel and driving
- Drink and drug abuse
- Passive world-watching, TV,
- Embellishment and over-production
- Over-long breaks, kitchen, canteen visits
- Reading irrelevant or nonsense material
- Interrupting others
- Daydreaming and doodling
- Silly emails and text messages
- Chat and gossip face-to-face and phone
- Unchallenged & unnecessary routines
- Shopping or buying for no purpose

Ideally, you should not be spending any time on these tasks as they eat up your time without contributing towards the achievement of your goals. Since these tasks are not important and urgent, these can be easily put off to another time. Ensure that you do not waste valuable time for these redundant tasks.

These are the four quadrants in the Eisenhower method. It is evident that this method can be used to sort your priority tasks and also decide the time to be allotted for each quadrant. Effective use of this method will help you ensure that your time is not invested on useless tasks. This method also enables you to finish all the priority tasks within the stipulated timeline.

POSEC Method

The POSEC method is an important as well as an effective time management tool. POSEC is the short form for prioritizing by Organizing, Streamlining, Economizing and Contributing.

Let us look at the five aspects of this principle in detail now.

Prioritizing:

Prioritizing means to put the things in your to-do list first. It is important that you prioritize your tasks based on their importance. This helps in ensuring that your time is not wasted on low priority tasks. You can prioritize your tasks based on the Maslow's theory of needs (which is explained in the next chapter of this book).

Organizing:

This aspect of this principle emphasizes on staying organized, which will help you in achieving your goals. It also deals with those tasks that you need to do on a regular basis to ensure that you progress towards the achievement of your goals. This organization of work will help you deal with your goals in a stable fashion despite all odds. This also involves the formulating of a plan for taking care of your essential needs such as clothing, shelter, food and safety etc.

Streamlining:

Sometimes, we all do things that we have to do though we may not like to do them. These tasks are required to go about your routine and cannot be avoided. Streamlining deals with those works and chores that need to be done on a daily basis. The streamlining aspect deals with automating those tasks that consume a lot of time and human efforts.

Economizing:

These tasks involve those things that one must do or would prefer doing. However, these tasks do not carry a tag of urgency with them. Hence, these tasks can be completed at a desired pace. Some examples of tasks that fall under this category are engaging in projects that you enjoy doing, acquiring new skills and engaging in tasks that ensure personal development. These tasks are usually associated with lower levels of priority.

Contributing:

Contribution is in the form of those tasks the benefits of which cannot be reaped immediately. However, the impact of these tasks can be seen in the long run. Examples of tasks that fall under these tasks are those that serve humanity such as acts of thoughtfulness and kindness.

The POSEC method helps you in improving your efficiency and helps you work better in a team. This method also helps the employer to come up with suitable goals for the employees, which will motivate them to achieve it. However, it is important that this method is executed with proper care to ensure that the employer reaps the maximum benefit out of it.

This method of time management also helps in breaking your macro or long term goals into short term ones. This helps in dealing with one minor goal at a time and completing them effectively. Another reason why this method of personal time management is universally favored is because it also takes into consideration your personal and social obligations, leisure activities apart from focusing on your priority tasks at workplace. In other words, this method ensures that there is proper work life balance. This is precisely why most people prefer this method of time management over the others.

Maslow's Theory of Needs

This theory was developed by Abraham Maslow, which deals with the motivation aspect of the human psychology. According to this theory, man's needs can be classified into one of the following categories:

1. Physiological needs

2. Safety needs

3. Love and belonging

4. Esteem

5. Self actualization

These needs are often depicted in the form of a pyramid with the physiological needs depicted in the bottom and the self actualization needs at the apex. Let us look at these needs in detail now.

Physiological needs

Physiological needs are those needs which are connected with human survival. In other words, these needs are the basic needs that need to be fulfilled for the existence of man such as food, water, shelter and clothing. These are highly important and need to be addressed first. This is precisely why these needs form the base of the Maslow's pyramid.

Safety needs

Once the physiological needs are taken care of, the next in line would be our safety needs. By safety, we don't just refer to the physical safety. The safety needs comprise of the following:

- ✓ Personal safety/security

- ✓ Financial safety/ security

- ✓ Health

- ✓ Safety/ security against accidents and other calamities

Why are these safety needs important? In the absence of these, one might end up being the victim of stress disorders and other psychological problems. Lack of economic security or job security will discourage an individual in putting their best efforts at work. Lack of good health can adversely impact one's performance at work. Therefore, these safety needs have to be given paramount importance once the physiological needs are satisfied and should not be looked at lightly.

Love and belonging

The third level in the pyramid of needs deals with the interpersonal needs of man and deals with one's sense of belongingness. This need is the most pronounced at times of childhood. According to Maslow, human beings require to be socially accepted and loved. This is the rationale behind man forming and becoming a part of social clubs and organizations. This is another reason why man believes in the system of family to derive the sense of belonging. Though this need is third on the hierarchy, this can gain more importance in certain cases if the peer pressure is too high.

Esteem

All of us want to be respected by the people around us. This need reflects man's desire to have self respect and self esteem. Esteem is nothing but the desire of human beings to be accepted and valued for what they are. An individual's performance at work place is an easy way to gain the respect of others. Some people take up hobbies to gain the acceptance of people.

According to Maslow, two versions of esteem needs exist. The lower version of esteem needs is characterized by the demand of respect from the people around them. This also includes the need for fame, status, recognition and attention. People with the lower version of esteem needs are often attention seeking in nature. The higher version of esteem needs deals with low levels of self esteem and demand self respect. The person with the higher version of esteem needs often feel the need for competence, independence, confidence, strength, freedom, mastery etc. According to Maslow, this higher version of esteem needs is more important than the lower version as the former is focused more on the inner competence of the individual as opposed to the latter. This inner competence can be improved only through positive experiences.

Self actualization needs

These needs form the apex of the pyramid. This level addresses the identification of the full potential of the individual and achieving the said full potential. According to Maslow, this level ascribes to the desire of man to achieve everything that he is capable of. To achieve this level, one is required to master the other levels of needs in the pyramid.

These are the five fundamental needs of mankind according to Maslow.

Time management and Maslow's theory

This theory of needs helps in identifying where we stand in terms of our needs. This theory is aimed at keeping the individual motivated at all points of time. Based on where one stands in terms of achieving the various levels of needs, priorities can be set to achieve the remainder of the needs. For instance, once the basic needs are addressed, man's efforts and time are spent on the other levels of needs. This adds a sense of direction and focus to one's efforts and in turn increases their efficiency. As we all know, increased efficiency means that lesser time is required to complete the same task without any errors.

Similarly, when you know where you stand in terms of the levels, you will have a clear idea of the time required to achieve the needs pertaining to that level. This will help you to plan accordingly and invest your time wisely. As such, this theory of needs plays an important role when it comes to time management.

Pomodoro Technique

The Pomodoro technique is another time management tool that was discovered in the late 1980s by Francesco Cirillo. According to this technique, work is broken down into intervals of twenty five minutes with the help of a timer. These intervals are separated by short breaks. These intervals of work are referred to as "pomodori" which is nothing but the plural term for tomato in Italian. This technique in built on the fact that the mental agility of an individual is tremendously improved by frequent breaks.

Implementation:

The implementation of this technique comprises of the following five steps:

Step One: Identify the task that needs to be done.

Step Two: Take the pomodoro timer and set the timer. Ideally, the timer is set to 25 minutes but you can change it to suit your needs.

Step Three: Keep working on the task till the timer rings. The timer will ideally ring once the twenty five minutes or the set time is over.

Step Four: Treat yourself to a small break. Make sure that this short break does not exceed four to five minutes. Taking long breaks can have a grave impact on your attention span and concentration levels.

Step Five: Once you have worked for four pomodori, treat yourself to a bigger break of fifteen to thirty minutes.

This technique comprises of different stages such as planning, tracking, recording, processing and visualizing. In the planning stage of this technique, a to-do list is prepared with an intention to identify the tasks to be completed for the day. This list also helps in identifying the efforts that require to be taken to achieve the tasks.

According to this task, any time spent over and above the pomodori is considered as the time spent for over learning. The inclusion of regular breaks is to aid in the assimilation of the data learnt or processed. Each pomodori is separated by a short interval. Four pomodori are believed to construe a set. A set is usually followed by a longer rest that is anywhere between fifteen to thirty minutes.

The ultimate aim of this technique is to ensure that the impact of internal as well as external disruptions when one sets out to work. The pomodori also brings in an element of utmost concentration and focus. When the timer is ticking, all that is there in our mind is to accomplish as much as possible before the timer rings. When the timer rings, the brain is trained to take a short break, which can be used to process the things learnt during the previous twenty five minutes. When the timer is set again, the human mind is trained to focus on the task in hand for the next twenty five minutes. In other words, this technique instills a sense of mental discipline. This in turn helps in increasing one's efficiency and productivity. The time spent for a given task is considerably reduced under this technique owing to the element of focus and direction associated with it.

Getting Things Done

Getting things done is another time management method that was discovered by David Allen, a productivity consultant. This method is famously known as the GTD method. According to this method, it is necessary to write down the important tasks and projects that we have planned inside our heads. In other words, it involves moving our ideas from inside our mind to an external surface like a notepad or a notebook. Upon recording these projects in a notepad, the next step would be to break them into smaller actionable points.

Our mind has the capacity to recall. However, this capacity will not work in our favor when we are working in haste or under a lot of stress. To avoid this, it is important that we do not recall too much on our memory, especially when it comes to important deliverables. Hence, writing them down somewhere will be easy to retrieve them and focus on them. This focus is much needed to complete these tasks.

Ideology behind GTD

According to David Allen, this method has two basic elements namely control and perspective. This method proposes a certain workflow process, which can be used to control all the commitments and tasks one wishes to get done within a stipulated time frame. The principle behind this method is to get all our goals out of our mind and record it somewhere. This is because, according to him, a person will be able to focus better and think better when his mind is not clogged with things. He will be able to take decisions with better clarity if his mind is clear to a certain extent. The clarity of the mind is required to focus on the below six aspects:

- ✓ **Current actions**: These are tasks that need to be completed immediately. This can be as simple as preparing for the meeting that is scheduled in the next hour. In other words, these are tasks that are lined up for you within the next few hours of the day. As you can see, these are really short term goals.
- ✓ **Current projects**: Current projects are nothing but the short term projects you are a part of. For instance, you may be a part of this project in your neighborhood that involves decorating the street for Christmas. These are again short term in nature and require your daily attention.
- ✓ **Areas of responsibility**: Areas of responsibility can be both short term as well as long term. But the key here is to focus on the short term responsibilities or rather the responsibilities that you have to do on a daily basis. For instance, if you are a student, it is your responsibility to finish your homework assigned for each day and focus on studying.
- ✓ **One to two years goals**: These are goals that can be achieved in the upcoming one or two years. This is when the shift happens from every day tasks to slightly bigger goals. An example of a goal that comes under this category can be to lose thirty pounds by the end of one year.

✓ **Three to five years life goals**: Once your goals for the next one year are decided, it is time for you to focus on the goals for the next three to five years. These goals are longer in duration and planning for them should start from today. For example, you may have a goal of getting a certain car by the end of three years. To own that car after three years, it is important that you start saving for it from today.

✓ **Long-term life goals**: As the name suggests, these are life goals. Once you have set your other goals, you will have more clarity in assessing where you want to be and what you want your life to be filled with in the long run. This clarity will help you fix your long-term goals. The duration of these goals is usually more than five years. An example of this goal would be to plan for your career if you are a student. If you are already employed, you can start planning for your retirement and start saving. These goals also require some action in the present to be able to achieve them in the long run.

Most theories tend to focus on the top- down approach. The top down approach is nothing but focusing on the long term goal and breaking it down into several smaller and short term goals. However, this method believes in the bottoms up approach. This is because, according to Allen, it is not possible for everyone to focus or visualize the bigger picture or the long term goal, especially when they are struggling every day to finish their tasks. The exercise of focusing and coming up with long term goals is lost here especially when you don't have any sort of control over your current state of affairs. When an individual takes control over the tasks or commitments lined up for the day, he will have both the time and clarity to look at the bigger picture. Hence this method focuses primarily on getting things done in the short term which will enable the individual to focus on the long term.

His method suggests the review of things on a weekly basis. While reviewing our progress and our goals, we tend to gain a new perspective, which should be used to set our priorities for the upcoming week. It is important that you set context for these weekly reviews. Merely going over the list of things completed will not do the trick. Group similar tasks together; for example, all the meetings that you had during the week can be clubbed together while all your phone calls may be clubbed together into another category. This will help us to review the tasks completed in an appropriate fashion.

GTD method proposes storing, tracking and retrieving the information pertaining to the tasks and commitments one has to complete. We often suffer from mental blocks when we don't have enough time to plan. This is why we should not rely too much on the memory capacity of our brain. This method tends to address these issues and suggests an effective system to record your goals and review them on a regular basis.

Workflow

As mentioned earlier, the GTD method suggests a certain workflow process. This workflow ideally consists of five important stages as follows:

✓ Capture

✓ Clarify

✓ Organize

✓ Reflect

✓ Engage

Accordingly, the first step in the workflow is to capture all the goals and commitments one has. Once you have captured all the essential things that need to be done, process what they are and what they represent. If you are of the opinion that a certain task can be discarded, score it off from your list. This is when you enter the second stage in the workflow. Upon clarifying, you will have a clear idea about each task on the list. You will have an exact figure on the tasks that require your action.

The third step in the workflow is to organize them accordingly. Group them into similar tasks. For example, all household chores can be clubbed together while errands that require you to go out can be clubbed separately. Prepare separate lists of similar activities.

The fourth step in the workflow is to reflect on our tasks. This is nothing but to review them from time to time. This review will serve as a reminder of the upcoming tasks and commitments. This will also help you identify those tasks that are yet to be completed. Update your lists after each review. This way, both your list as well as your mind is clear from things that have already been completed and entire focus can be on the things that require completion.

The fifth and final step in the workflow is to engage. This simply means putting your plan into action. Look at your lists and start working on them with confidence and energy.

Hence this method helps us to focus on the things that need to be done in the short run thereby preparing us for the tasks that need to be completed in the long run.

Chapter 4: The 80/20 Principle in Time Management

The 80/20 rule is famously known as the Pareto principle. This is also known as the Rule of the Vital Few. According to this principle, there is a huge imbalance between the efforts that go into every task and the outcomes. In other words, it is not necessary that your efforts will be converted into results in the same proportion. You might wonder how this is relevant to time management. In this chapter, we shall see how the Pareto principle can be extended to time management.

Pareto Principle in Time Management

The Pareto principle is applicable to time management in the following aspects:

80% of the tasks produce only 20% of the results:

The tasks that we undertake on a daily basis fall into either of the two categories:

- ✓ 80% of the tasks that have a minimal impact on our lives

- ✓ 20% of the tasks that have a major impact on our lives

This means that not all the tasks that we undertake on a day are highly important. According to this principle, your efficiency is determined by the 20% of the tasks assigned for the day. In other words, 20 percent of the tasks in your to-do list are more important than the 80 percent of the tasks. The key is to identify those tasks that have a major impact and focus on them. This way, you will reduce the time spent on 80% of the tasks that have a very minimal impact on us and will help us focus better on the tasks that have a major impact. This sense of direction ensures that we do not miss out on the most important tasks for the day while trying to focus on the other things that require completion by the end of the day.

80% Of Your Work Can Be Completed In 20% Of Your Working Hours When You Are Focused:

Most of us struggle through deadlines because we find it difficult to stay focused for a long time. Our concentration constantly wavers. This lack of attention results in you taking up more time than required to finish a given task. These constant distractions eat up your time without your knowledge and ends up affecting your productivity as well. The accuracy of the work done depends highly on the level of concentration you possess at the time of doing the job. When your concentration is compromised, it is clear that the quality of your work is also gravely compromised.

On the other hand, when your day is devoid of any distractions, it is easier to finish most of your work in a short span of time. Allocate approximately 20% of your working hours to focus on priority projects and tasks. Since these priority tasks are more important than the other menial jobs, it is important that you give your complete attention to these jobs. You can get a great deal of work done in this time since there are no distractions.

80% Of The Interruptions/Distractions Can Be Avoided While The Remaining 20% Can Be Controlled:

So many factors contribute to the many distractions that may come our way when we try to work or study. These distractions are the sole reasons behind us not completing the work within the stipulated time. These can be in the form of a phone call from your friend or your favorite movie playing in the T.V. Most people consider distractions as unavoidable aspects of their lives. However, this is not true. It is entirely possible to avoid as well as control distractions, if you make the conscious effort to do so.

In the later part of this book, we have suggested tips to manage distractions or interruptions. Going by those tips, you will be able to avoid at least 80% of the interruptions. Though the remainder 20% of the distractions may not be avoided completely, they can be controlled in such a fashion that their impact on your concentration levels is minimal.

80% Of What Is Filed Is Never Referred Again.

We often spend a lot of time to file documents laboriously for future reference purposes. Apart from filing, we spend equal amounts of time in maintaining these physical folders to ensure that the documents do not get damaged. The harsh truth is that we refer only 20% of these documents in the future. Instead of filing everything and trying to make room for the additional paper work, the best solution would be to file only those papers that have legal or financial implications and based on their utility at a future date.

80% Of The Business Profits Come From 20% Of The Clients:

Two common misconceptions that are prevalent among people who are new to business is that all clients are important and all clients deserve equal attention. Have you wondered how certain businesses cater to only a certain class of people and yet succeed? This is because they have identified those clients who are assets to the business. Not all clients are beneficial to the business in the same way. Instead of spending a lot of time on low profile clients, the same time can be invested on the handful of clients who bring more profits to the business. If you look at it, only 20% of the entire client base requires your maximum attention. The rest 80% of the clientele contribute to only 20% of your business and does not require your maximum attention. Hence the key to success is to focus on those selected clients and reap the maximum benefits out of it instead of slogging to match the expectations of all the clients.

20% Of The Clothes We Own Are Worn By Us 80% Of The Time:

Most of us have the habit of buying new clothes even before our old clothes become worn out. Let us not forget the tempting sales that happen once in a while where we make it a point to stack our wardrobes with new clothes.

But the problem does not lie there. It arises when we don't discard the old clothes as we keep piling the new ones. We end up spending hours trying to de-clutter our wardrobes to make room for clothes and for discarding old clothes. How often have we been late to an interview because we were fishing out our lucky tie from our bursting wardrobe? How often have we spent hours trying to dig out our favorite shirt from the ever growing pile of clothes? This time can be saved if you identify the 20% of the clothes that you wear often and sort the remaining 80% accordingly. It is a proven fact that we tend to wear only 20% of our clothes on a regular basis, either to college or work. Identify those clothes. Stack them neatly in the top shelves of your wardrobes where it is easier to retrieve. This can save a lot of time as well as human efforts, especially when you are running on a tight schedule.

From the above instances, it is clear that the 80/20 principle can be applied for pretty much everything that involves the element of time. At times, we are swamped with overwhelming work and demands. Instead of taking it all up and slogging, identify that 20% of the tasks that will make a difference as opposed to the 80% of the menial tasks that can be done easily by anyone. This not only saves a lot of your time but also improves your efficiency.

Every time before you take up any work, ask yourself this question – "Does this task belong to the insignificant 80% or the significant 20%?" You can decide the course of action based on the answer. An important catch here is that this 20% need not be same for two people who do the same set of activities every day. What you perceive as important and significant may not considered as important by the other person. However, you cannot cross off the Pareto principle as a completely subjective approach as the priorities are determined based on external factors as well.

Chapter 5: Guide to Time Management

In this chapter, we have listed out the various steps that can help you manage your time effectively.

Set your goals:

It is important that we have set clear and achievable goals. These goals can be short term as well as long term. Why are goals important? Goals add a sense of direction and purpose to your life. When there is direction and purpose, our efforts are more refined. When our efforts are more refined, we end up accomplishing a lot in less time. This is precisely why goals are important.

If you are someone who's never good with setting goals, you can begin by setting goals daily and then build on it from there. These goals can be as specific as they can get. Once the habit of goal setting has set in, this can be used effectively to set long term goals.

Goal setting has two important facets namely prioritizing and staying focused. Let us look at them in detail:

Prioritize your tasks

As mentioned earlier, many of us run behind deadlines and finish it only in the last minute. This is not because we don't have enough time to do the tasks but because we don't plan our time properly. You need to have a proper plan for the day to plan your time. We end up wasting time usually because we seldom have a set agenda for the day or the week.

Setting goals help us in understanding what tasks need to be completed on a priority basis. Understanding the priority of the things that need to be done will motivate us not to waste time or put it off for some other time. Listing out things on the basis of priority can throw light on what needs to be done next.

Staying Focused

An important thing about setting goals is staying focused at all times. Lack of focus will deter you from achieving your goals, both short term as well as long term. Sometimes, we tend to lose focus when there are too many goals. For instance, you have set ten goals for the day. If for instance, a single goal takes a lot of time to finish, you might end up with limited time to accomplish the remaining nine goals. The long list of unaccomplished goals might end up adding to your list of worries and you lose focus.

Another reason why we lose focus is that we are not completely aware of our goals or priorities. This can be easily resolved by glancing at our To-do list. At the same time, understand the purpose behind each goal and why each goal is important. When you realize the rationale behind each goal of yours, focus comes into play automatically.

Schedule Your Time

Once done with setting your goals or priorities, allocate specific time to tasks to ensure tasks don't overlap. Frequent interruptions, endless meetings, and urgent tasks, make is all too easy to get confused or skip important tasks. In some instances, you can be so busy that eventually, you fail to accomplish highly prioritized goals and projects. For this and other related reasons, you need to know how to schedule your time.

To schedule your time, you can use several tools the easiest of which is a pen and paper. Others include, but are not limited to apps and software such as MS Outlook, Google Calendar, and Business Calendar. Find the right tool that suits your budget, personal taste, current job structure, and your personal situation.

How to Become an Effective Time Manager

Once you have decided on a scheduling tool, schedule your time in the following manner:

Be Aware Of the Available Time

The best approach to cultivating awareness of available time is to start by designating work time i.e. the time you want to avail to your work depending on your work goals and the nature of your job. If you are pushing for a promotion for instance, you may want to put in more hours at work to show your dedication to the company or firm. On the other hand, if you are looking to spare time for out-of-work activities, you will want to stick to your dedicated work hours, with no extension.

Schedule Important Actions

Schedule the actions you must undertake to do a good job. For example, if you are a manager, set enough time to deal with team members' personal issues, supervision, and coaching needs.

Time Management

Schedule Top Priority Tasks First

Go through your To-do-list and schedule to first urgent and high priority activities, including essential maintenance errands you cannot avoid or delegate. Let the completion of these tasks appear at the time you are most productive during the day.

Allocate Contingency Time

Allocate extra time in your schedule to deal with the emergencies and contingencies. You can judge from past experience how much time to allow for the unforeseen, and emergencies.

Plan for Your Discretionary Time

The extra space left in your planner is the available time to achieve your goals and deliver your priorities. Go through your personal goals and prioritized to do list, analyze the time needed to achieve them and then schedule them in.

Analyze Your Tasks

If you find that there is little or no time left for discretionary activities after scheduling your planner, go back through the previous steps and determine whether all the tasks outlined are an absolutely necessity. You may find some tasks can be handled in a more time efficient manner, or delegated.

Create a Weekly Schedule

A weekly schedule should help display your planned time-slots and all activities you intend to engage in for the week. The schedule should help you explain and justify the need to prioritize tasks, and the need to allocate time to addressing the unforeseen. When creating your weekly schedule, use logic and sensibility to slot in task, taking advantage of lunch breaks or other 'free' times to accomplish personal goals.

Generate your first weekly activity schedule; doing so will motivate you to keep going and help you realize which tasks and time slots often repeat weekly or monthly.

A Sample Weekly Time Slot Manager

An example of a weekly time slot manager may look like this:

Monday

AM

1. Check emails

2. Project time-slot

3. Staff matters arising time-slot

4. Staff appraisal 1

5. Check emails

PM

1. Return phone calls

2. Emergencies time-slot

3. Reading monthly reports

4. Appraisals preparation

5. Check emails and initial responses

Tuesday

AM

1. Check emails, post, initial response.

2. Review last week reports

3. Department meeting

4. Agency meeting

5. Check emails

PM

1. Customer visit

2. Customer visit

3. Appraisal preparation

4. Check emails

5. Phone calls and correspondence

Wednesday

AM

1. Check emails

2. Appraisal preparation

3. Staff appraisal

4. Staff appraisal

5. Check emails

PM

1. Supplier visit 1

2. Supplier visit 2

3. Major phone calls

4. Check emails

5. Thinking time-slot for new strategy project

Thursday

AM

1. Check emails.

2. Chase figures for weekly report

3. Strategy meeting

4. Process review time-slot

5. Check emails

PM

1. Emergencies time-slot

2. Systems and process review time-slot

3. Weekly report preparation

4. Check emails

Friday

AM

1. Check emails

2. Weekly report

3. Conference planning

4. Unresolved non-urgent issues

5. Phone calls

6. Check emails

PM

1. Agenda for next week department meeting

2. Plan next week's schedule

3. Spare time-slot for staff issues

4. Check emails

5. Clear up outstanding issues

Create a Productive Morning Routine

There is no official time for when a morning should start since you may wake up earlier or later in the day. That said, research has shown that productivity is usually very high in the mornings; thus, it is important that you aim to accomplish more in the mornings.

This makes a morning routine a very vital part of effective time management as well as productivity. While you may creating an effective morning routine as a challenge, there is no ideal morning routine. Surprised? No need to be. Truth be told, all of us have different things that we feel are important to accomplish in the morning. For instance while cleaning may be your most important task, someone else may hold a morning jog or any other exercise activity as his or her most important task or activity.

Mornings are the perfect time to be creative, exercise, as well as have some personal time. To top this up, science has indicated that your will power is strongest in the morning; this means you can easily accomplish difficult tasks that instigate procrastination if you tackle them in the mornings.

Because of this, how you spend your morning is also a precursor to how your day shall progress. Consider this: a calm and productive morning will yield calmness and productivity throughout the day, while a hectic morning ritual will result into fatigue or stress during the day.

Simply put, creating a powerful and effective morning routine will ensure that you have the energy and right mental attitude to work effectively throughout your day. When you manage your morning well, you should also see a boost in productivity and in so doing, boost your motivation and the day's earnings.

How to Create an Effective Morning Routine

That said; let us see how you can make your mornings more productive.

Make Priorities Easier

It does not matter what task you want to prioritize. What matters is that the task you choose to prioritize and complete in the morning increases your productivity and saves you time. How can you achieve this? For instance, if your jogging is your morning priority, place your workout clothes in an easy to access place. If your morning priority is working on your project, ensure to place all materials relative to that project are in one area the night before.

Make Exercise a Priority

Who said that regular exercise is an athletes' only thing? Exercising in the morning effectively boosts your mood, as well as giving you a radiance energy that will last you the whole day. For most people, engaging in a cardio workout works to clear a clogged mind and boost focus. Dedicate a minimum of 20 minutes of your morning ritual to exercise.

Plan In Advance

Do not just wait for the morning to come before deciding how to spend it. At the end of your day, create a plan on what you aim to accomplish in the coming day, and write down all the tasks you need to complete in the morning. Ensure to plan the most challenging activities or tasks first; as research has shown, accomplishing tasks that require a lot of will power in the morning improves your productivity and mood.

After creating your list, set it up somewhere you can view it first thing in the morning, and make sure to follow your plan for the day. To create some order to your mornings, routinely practice this morning ritual. However, avoid rushing around the room looking for things or items you need in the morning. Choose your day's outfit before getting into bed, and place cell phone, keys, or other items you need in the morning in a visible place within easy reach.

Create a Grace Period

Allow a grace period of 15 minutes before getting into tasks or important responsibilities. If you have a pre-planned morning schedule created the day before, you will be able to manage your morning time better.

Creating a grace period can afford you the luxury of never being late in getting to work or being late for any meeting. For instance, a grace period of say 10-15 minutes time can help you arrive for a meeting with grace and dignity. This is a bigger benefit compared to the shame you would have felt if you rushed into the meeting and still got to be 15-20 minutes late.

Try a Jawbone Wrist's Vibration

This could appear as a rather weird advice that would probably work well on movie screens or virtual world. However, as opposed to using an ordinary alarm clock, try a Jawbone that gently vibrates on your wrist in a bid to wake you up "instantly".

The biggest temptation that an alarm clock poses is to hit the snooze button and continue with sleep. In effective time management and productivity, the snooze button is not your friend. It cuts in on had pre-planned time. Contrary to what people think and believe, not many people are very fond of waking up particularly during chilly morning weather.

Relax in the Evening

In these hard economic times, it is harder to manage time if stress in the workplace is taking a toll on you. While it is not possible to completely eliminate stress, learning how to relax after a long and stressful day is vital to a productive morning.

How to relax After a Long Day's Work

If you find it hard to relax after a hard day's work, you may benefit from the following tips:

Give Your Mind a Break

Most of us tend to carry thoughts of unfinished tasks home. However, this tends to cause even more stress. Dealing with stress involves mental and physical conscious efforts. Learn to separate your work from your family. Forget about your coworkers and your boss the instant you leave the office, and spend time with your partner and children. There is a lot more to life than work.

Take a Warm Shower

A warm bath can help you sleep better after a long, tiring day at work. Warm water drains all your stress, helps you forget about work, and experience the soothing effect of the water on your body. By taking a warm shower, you will wake up refreshed and full of energy to accomplish your planned schedule for the day.

Read Your Favorite Book

This is a good way to relax and forget about your work problems. However, choose a soft bound or hard cover book, rather than an eBook reader or a tablet as the radiation emitted by these devices can obstruct sleep.

Meditate or Exercise

There are different forms of meditational exercises such as transcendental meditation, Tai chi, and Yoga that can help you relax and help you connect with what matters most in life.

If practiced a few minutes before sleeping, Meditation is very effective and effectively helps you wake up refreshed. To relieve stress, why not try exercising. When you exercise, your body produces feel good hormones that help you feel relaxed. The exercise you engage in could be as simple as walking or riding a bike; the exercise does not matter that much; what matters is that you enjoy it and regularly engage in it. By so doing, you can fight stress, anxiety, and all its adjacent symptoms.

That said, you do not have to leave your home compound to exercise. This is so because gardening is a form of exercise that does not require you to leave your home and that works extremely well. While gardening involves a degree of physical activity, the mental benefits of plants and nature can help you eliminate stress on a deeper level.

Set Boundaries and Learn To Say No

As part of managing time, sometime, you may have to make snap decisions especially in emergencies or impromptu meetings. Unfortunately, most of us tend to agree to every suggestion in a bid to appear 'human'. However, not all snap decisions require an affirmative action. Actually, it is better to give a polite NO and avoid pushing yourself into an extreme situation.

Did you know that even the kindest people say no? Learning to say no is an effective tool guaranteed to help you cut out the less important activities in your life, and focus on your most important activities. To sharpen your time management skills, learn to set boundaries and say no.

It is also very important that you develop an acute ability to differentiate between important and urgent task. Setting boundaries will help you know when you cross them and help you not to cross them. It will help you curtail the temptation to say yes when what you actually want to say is no! Here is the kicker; in case you say yes when what you meant was no, you may spend hours, days, and sometimes months regretting the "yes" decision. You will feel a lot of resentment while wondering why you said yes in the first place.

Learn to say no even if such a response brings about feelings of shame and sometimes guilt; a good example is when you have to say no to your children. Though this is a perfectly natural response, majority of parents fear that their children may consider them unloving or without any feelings for them.

Setting boundaries and learning to say no is about prioritizing and having the courage to love yourself and say no even at the risk of disappointing others. When faced with different scenarios on a day-to-day basis, learning to say no will help you filter out the unimportant. On the other hand, by saying no, you will gain enough time to deal with the important aspects of your life, and in so doing, boost your productivity.

How to Set Boundaries and Say No

That said, saying no, or setting boundaries for loved ones and authority figures is often difficult. After realizing that you cannot say no to everything, then the following guidelines can help you sharpen your skills to draw boundaries:

Maintain a Journal

Maintaining a journal is very important especially in cases where you feel resentful that you failed to set boundaries and possibly said yes instead of NO. When you are feeling resentful, write this down, and note all the times that you experience this. This can help you to recognize which situations make you feel the most resentment.

Practice It

Saying no is a skill that develops over time, but like everything else, you have to practice. There are individuals in our lives whom we cannot instantaneously say no to. In these instances, it helps to start small; start by saying no to small matters that concern you, and then move on to smaller matters that concern other people. When you are sure you are going to say yes to someone you really want to say no to, it helps a lot to have a mantra.

A mantra is simply a phrase you use to remind yourself of your inner strength. An effective way to practice a mantra is to have a ring, bracelet, or necklace that you can stroke when the desire to say yes overwhelms you. Tailor the mantra to your difficulty to say no.

If you have a lot of difficulty saying no, choose a strong mantra that helps you choose discomfort over resentment. An example of how to say no to an extra serving during mealtimes is, "my plate is full" or "sorry I cannot take that on right now". In simple terms, choose something that adds more power to your resolve, such as "I can say no". A mantra does not necessarily have to be a chant; it can be anything, as long as what you choose empowers you.

Setting boundaries will help you determine what is, and what is not important, and will help you achieve more in the areas of your life that matter. Setting boundaries also requires that you set up a schedule that you can follow. A schedule should not be too restrictive and should afford you some flexibility.

Reject Unnecessary Requests

This is important when you have too much to do, and too little time. Learn to say "No" to unimportant requests or additional tasks that can overwhelm you and cause stress. The sad thing is that a majority of us cannot manage to say "No" because we think it makes us appear rude and self-centered; we think saying no will trigger conflict, rejection, or miss an important opportunity. However, be aware that barriers of this nature are self-created; as such, you can easily overcome them by adopting a friendlier tone. Adopt a few humble expressions such as:

"I'd love to do this, but ..."

"I'm quite busy now. Can you ask me again at...?"

Set Deadlines for All Tasks

Irrespective of whether tasks are urgent, important, or not urgent, setting deadlines for the completion of tasks gives you a timeline for the completion of tasks, and helps you prepare for unforeseen emergencies.

However necessary this may be, do not set deadlines at the expense of your health or well-being. You do not have to overwork yourself, or physically or mentally fatigued to meet a deadline. Taking a short break, say a 5 minutes' walk can help you get fresh air and clear your mind. That said, set deadlines for every task!

How to Set Deadlines

Although setting deadlines may pose a challenge at first, the following tips can help you be ahead of the schedule at all times.

Allocate More Time To 'A' Tasks.

If you have set aside one hour for a walk, it might be better to cut down on that time and allocate a portion of it to something far more important. Sometimes, you may have to delegate and have someone complete tasks on your behalf. Hiring someone to do it for you may cost a few bucks, but it is worth it, considering the extra time it gives you in working towards that important pitch towards a new client.

Accomplish Tasks Even When Deadlines "Bite"

Some tasks can take longer than you actually planned for; In case you feel that you will be unable to complete a task in more time than you had desired; don't tense! In these instances, a majority of us make the mistake of reducing our work speed, or just shelving the task so as to re-allocate more time for the task, or completely re-schedule the task. Working in one-spirit helps you met deadlines even in instances where you are pressed for time.

Plan for It

Research shows that making a 'plan of action' can give greater fluidity to how you approach a task. Planning, even if mentally done for a few seconds, can go a long way in ensuring that you finish the task at hand in the 'time limit' you have set to achieve it. Furthermore, planning will clear your mind of doubts on your ability to complete the task within the set deadline. Planning helps you become organized, and gives you clarity, two things you need to manage time and become more productive.

Assess Time for Each Activity

You do not need rocket science to approximate time needed to accomplish day-to-day tasks such as cleaning, eating dinner, or going for a walk. When you review your daily To-do-list, make a mental assessment of how much time it will take to complete each task.

Write this time estimate next to the task to help manage your time better and boost productivity. For instance, if you spend 1-2 hours on a task that would normally take 45 minutes, the extra wasted time may cause delays in the completion of other tasks. Be realistic about the amount of time you allocate to each task without over working yourself.

Weigh Your Options

Whether time is bad, or you have pressing deadlines that scare you, remember, you always have a choice. Sometimes, the desperation to complete work task may emanate from biting far too much that you can handle. Thus, it is important to reassess our goals and only allocate 'realistic' amounts of work to the realistically available time.

Do Not Work Beyond Time "Limits"

Everyone has a particular duration of time where you can work without fatigue or distress, commonly referred to as your 'productive' time. Research shows that most people work well within an 8 to 10 hour time timeline. Beyond that, you are just working yourself towards exhaustion. After the 8-10 hours timeline, you will not really get your work done as well as you would were you to approach it with a fresh mind the next morning. On the contrary, after working for more than 10 hours, you will go home tired and possibly easily irritable.

Acknowledge Distractions

Everyone would like to work flawlessly, but the fact of the matter is, distractions are an integral part of humanity. While working on a particular task, your mind might wander to unrelated tasks or tasks you are yet to begin work on, thus neglecting the current task. Though it is human to be distracted, you need to focus on one task, and limit multi-tasking.

Do Things One Step at A Time

The rule of thumb is to break down goals into smaller components so you can manage them better. A majority of those who adopt a 'step-by-step' approach on every occasion often report dealing with common anxieties and "rush-hour" problems, something very common with urgent tasks.

How to Avoid Distractions and Accomplish One Thing at a Time

Though it may appear difficult in the beginning, it is possible to shelve all other tasks and jobs and focus on a single undertaking. Studies show that our minds cannot focus on many things at once. That notwithstanding; here is how to take on difficult tasks one-step at a time.

Start Easy

Common sense dictates that, to beat deadlines, you do not have make your initial steps too difficult. Start easy, and gradually ease into the work at hand. Over time, you will gradually gain more "strength" and be able to take on tasks that are more difficult. Your tasks do not have to be of equal intensity. However, you should set realistic goals for all tasks. Allow yourself time to get settled in, start small, and in no-time, the entire project should gradually begin to fall into place.

Regularly Review Your Goals

Time experts say that you should review your goals at every step of the way in a bid to confirm that you are on track. Due to the unpredictability of most events, you never can tell when things have gone awry until it is too late, which signals a big failure.

As you review your goals, readjust ideas or projects in accordance with the unforeseen changes that come your way. Assess the situation in its entirety, making sure to accommodate any changes that might have come along since the start of your project.

Reason Things Out

You may rush to complete a certain task within a given deadline, but lack of enough thought can jeopardize the whole project and result in time wastage. Unfortunately, many of us often go about completing tasks in a mechanical manner, without giving thought to how to go about them at all.

Before performing each little step, for a moment, think of the best possible way to go about performing each step. Try to look at the matter this way: if you've already invested time thinking of the various steps required to complete your project, why not spend a few minutes thinking of how to approach each step? It is common knowledge that it is better to be prepared rather than rushing into something with a blank mind.

Look Back and Review Your Progress

Most tasks require a consecutive systematic approach that demands that every step be done right. That means when you find yourself stuck in a particular step, it probably means you have not quite completed the last step as required. Though it may appear as delaying your progress, it is not a bad idea to look back and review your current endeavors. It is better to do this now rather than discovering that you have made several mistakes soon after completing a project.

Be Committed

To get out of your 'comfort zone' and make progress in becoming a better time manager, a strong commitment is necessary.

How to Become, and Remain Committed

As we have indicated, commitment is very important, below are the simple, actionable steps on how to commit to tasks:

Appreciate Your Obligations

As demanding as your obligations and goals may appear, be aware that you have to do what it takes to complete them. Serious commitments may at times demand skipping those weekly parties and family re-unions without regret or feeling the need to quit. Also, make sure you are meeting deadlines and completing goals on time and that you are not diverting from your original obligation or plan. Here is the truth: doing something well demands a lot of dedication and commitment.

Strive To Work Hard

Success does not come around seeking for you; to achieve success, you have to get out of your comfort zone, and get thing done. As the saying goes, a spark may start a fire, but it takes a fire to start a bonfire. To achieve success in your tasks and goals, be self-driven from the heart and mind, and work against the odds to achieve your dreams. Understand that disappointments and failures are part of life, but often go away with time. Realize that difficult moments are tests, which if you endure, you will garner the courage to defeat all odds and achieve your desired dreams or goals. Never let anything stop you from having that 'desire': the desire to make it in life.

Create a Visual Blueprint

All dreams start in the mind where they are visualized and later turned into a reality. Jot down your dream onto a piece of paper and take necessary steps to actualize them. If you are really committed to seeing your dreams turn into reality, make sure not to skip this crucial step. To remain committed to something, you must exhibit commitment, which often begins with visualization.

Have a Positive Approach

One way to ensure the realization of your dreams is to avoid negative people who normally bring you down with their lack of self-worth. You could be having a wonderful idea that the world desperately needs, but negativity from those around it can kill it altogether. Instead of hanging around negative people, look for like-minded friends, use positive affirmations, and commit yourself to positivity. Only through positivity do grand dreams begin to come true.

Be Organised

Being organized has a lot to do with your daily scheduling. Since you have already determined your long-term goal and have established your guideposts, the next step is to implement an action plan that helps you effectively manage your time. You can then implement your action plan using short-term goals. If your aim is not to make radical changes, but rather, to eliminate daily stress, the time you use to set your goals is enough to set your priorities in order.

If you have to refocus on your goals, then you will need organize your goals in a manner where addressing short-term goals leads to the achievement of the bigger picture or long term goals. Write down short-term actions you need to take to realize a long-term goal. If you find the tasks somehow overburdening, you may have to seek the services of an assistant, or simply break down the tasks to make what needs doing doable.

How to Become Organized

That said, through the simple steps below, becoming and staying organized becomes a breeze:

Prepare

You have to admit that there is nothing more stressful and time consuming than being unprepared. Spend some time creating your To-do list, and cleaning up before you leave.

If you have everything covered up (in terms of preparation), you are less likely to fret about work when night comes. After you get to work the following morning, you will be relaxed, in total control, and be in a position to handle things as they come. Being prepared sets a positive tone for your day, and allows you to accomplish more with your time.

Manage Your Time

It is a fact; you cannot manage everything unless you create easy to follow schedules. Begin by creating a list of what needs completion in order of priority. Categorize the list based on what you should do personally and what you can delegate. Note tasks that need immediate completion, those that need completion before day end, for next week, or forthcoming week.

The key here is to classify or manage big tasks into manageable tasks spread over time, and delegating task that do not demand your personal attention. When managing your time, create buffer times where you can address emergency or unexpected tasks. Also, have some time to relax and restore your well-being.

Adopt Tickler Files

Obtain about 90 file folders; say white ones numbered 1 through 30, blue ones numbered 1 through 30 and red ones numbered 1 through 30. These numbering should represent the current month, the next month, and the month after that. Supposing you need to follow up with a client on a particular deal, say next month, you can take your client's piece of handwritten tickler file and prop it into the blue file folder that's labeled 10.

Even if you forget about the deal, the tickler should pop up all by itself on the said 10th day of next month and get you to be aware of it. Tickler files when used right should help you reduce clutter, and let you organize your daily activities, while avoiding the temptation to forget or skip matters. Tickler files can work better than pads, computers, or phones that could outshine the file folders in the drawer. The tickler file system should work when adopted as manual, automated, virtual, physical, or hybrid method.

Block Your Time

Forget the lock-in-stone appointments that majority of us use; you can choose to make your version that features pre-located, locked-in-stone appointments with yourself and the work to be accomplished. Every year, we lock down months ahead. For instance, you can clump many of your important phone appointments during a month in one day and book a Phone Day in each month a year ahead.

Each month to the next, book many work appointments, coaching meetings, speaking engagements, time blocs for works and for writing your monthly newsletters on a book. Your objective should be to occupy your schedule with very little unassigned time as possible. If you are able to lay your calendar out before you and block or pre-assign most of your time in advance, only a little amount of time will go to waste. Block time for high priority tasks to prevent others and their demands from causing a reschedule of important tasks on you To-do-list or appointments.

Looking at the bigger picture:

Often we overlook certain crucial things during the course of the day that could play an important role in achieving our goals. These little things can end up saving your time. Sometimes, we tend to simplify our goals and their purposes and not allocate enough time for accomplishing each. Hence looking at the bigger picture will always help us to prioritize and work efficiently.

How Is It Done?

You might wonder as to how you can create or look at the bigger picture. Let me explain. For instance, if you are a student, you can prepare a calendar for the different activities, assignments and tests that are due that month. You can extend this exercise towards preparing a calendar for the entire semester. This will help you keep a track of all the important deadlines you have in the upcoming weeks and prioritize your work. Similarly, it will help you realize how your daily goals are in tandem with the macro goals for the semester, thereby making you regard them as important as the macro goals themselves.

On the other hand, if you are working, you can make a calendar for the important meetings and discussions for the month and keep updating it as and when required. This will bring in a lot more perspective to your work as you will be paying more attention to it in an attempt to prepare yourself for the meetings. This not only saves your time but also increases your efficiency and productivity.

One important advantage of looking at the bigger picture is that you will stop procrastinating beyond a point. As you might have noticed, your daily goals are linked to your goals for the month. As and when you keep putting off your daily goals, achieving your macro goals will become a tedious task and kicks off the panic alarm. This realization perhaps will deter you from putting off everyday's work.

Review

It is not important if you just prepare a calendar. Keep reviewing it on a regular basis. You will be able to analyze where time has been wasted and how better you can make up for the lost time in the upcoming days. Reviewing also helps you to allocate enough time for leisure activities.

It's that time of the day!

Each of us is productive at different times of the day. If you are a morning person, then perhaps early morning might be that time of the day when you are the most efficient. On the other hand, if you are a late riser, you are the most productive in the later part of the day. In other words, contrary to popular belief, everybody is the most efficient at some point of time during the day, irrespective of how lazy they are.

How to identify

Identifying the best time of your day is pretty simple. Analyze how your energy levels are throughout the day. Pay close attention to how your attention span varies throughout the day. Understanding your sleep cycles also help you a great deal in this exercise.

Why is it important

When we understand the best time of the day, we can utilize that time to finish the high priority tasks that require our maximum concentration and energy. We will also consciously make an effort to not waste the productive hours of the day this way.

Parcels of time

It is not humanely possible to work continuously for hours at a stretch. Even if it is possible, the accuracy of the work and the efficiency of the person will not be consistent throughout. So break your time into smaller parcels and work.

Say you have a task on hand that requires at least two hours of your time to finish. Instead of sitting on the work for two hours at a stretch, you can work for thirty minutes first. Take a break and then sit on the task again. This way, you are resting enough in such a way that your efficiency doesn't get affected.

Why is it important that you micromanage your time in this fashion? When you divide your time into smaller parcels, you will be aware of how efficiently you have spent every minute. For instance, you have a chapter to study and you have allotted two hours for it. When you divide the two hours into smaller parcels of fifteen minutes, you will be able to track effectively how quickly you are studying every fifteen minutes. You will also be able to analyze if your concentration is slipping away and take a break accordingly. This way, you are fixing issues pertaining to concentration immediately as opposed to realizing that you were not able to concentrate effectively at the end of two hours.

How to do it

Now that you have prepared a calendar for the entire month highlighting the important deadlines and discussions, you can start micromanaging your time on an hourly as well as on a daily basis. Say you have an important meeting coming up in the next week. You can spend at least an hour every day preparing the presentation instead of sitting up for seven hours the night before the meeting.

Similarly, if you have to study four subjects, instead of studying the same subject for one day, you could divide the studying hours among the four subjects in a day. This will break the monotony of studying the same subject the entire day.

Hence the key is divide your time and focus on each parcel of time at a time.

Balance your efforts

If you are done with the goals for the day sooner than you thought, use the extra time to finish off some menial tasks that you had assigned for tomorrow. This way, you wouldn't be working hard one day and be completely idle the next day. Try to achieve some consistency when it comes to the amount of efforts that goes into everyday's work. This way, your mind and body is prepared for a set amount of work every day.

Take a break

People are often under the misconception that taking a break is a waste of time. On the contrary, taking a break can help you manage your time and increase your efficiency. Take a short break between sessions of studying or working. The key is to decide how much time you are allocating for these breaks beforehand. For instance, if you decide to take a ten minutes break every one hour, ensure that you stick to the ten minutes break. Do not extend it unless it is absolutely necessary.

Taking breaks is important for the following reasons:

- ✓ It gives you an opportunity to relax after a strenuous session of studying or working.

- ✓ You will be motivated to work well if you have a break to look forward to.

- ✓ Your mind gets refreshed and becomes prepared to work after a short break.

- ✓ You can use the break to review how much you have covered so far.

Some of the Do's and Don'ts when it comes to taking breaks are as follows:

- ✓ Do allocate a reasonable time limit for the break and stick to it.

- ✓ Do ensure that the time allotted for the break is proportionate to the time spent for working. For example, if you work for an hour, ensure that the break is for not more than ten minutes.

- ✓ Understand that you will need more breaks if you intend to work for longer hours.

- ✓ In case, you are just going to take a nap or a walk during your break time, make sure that you have an alarm or a beeper in place to let you know when the ten minutes is over.

✓ Do get up from your place and stretch for a few minutes during your break time. This ensures that you don't end up with a stiff neck or a sore back that will in turn affect your productivity.

✓ Try to engage in small activities during your break that will help in increasing your energy levels. It could be a quick stroll around the house or some power jogging or any other activity that is physically stimulating.

✓ Don't engage in activities that are time consuming during your breaks. For instance, don't sit to watch the T.V. while you are taking a break. You will not notice the ten minutes slipping away.

✓ Do not log into any social networking sites while you are taking a break as we all know that ten minutes is just not enough to catch up on stuff.

Vacations

Just like how you require breaks on a daily basis, it is important that you take a brief break from work and go on a vacation. These vacations can be the stress reliever that you might have been waiting for. A solid vacation is capable of giving you a fresh perspective and renewed energy that can be used to increase your productivity. It can also increase your motivation to work. Ensure that you go on a vacation at the right time and not during the busiest time of the year for your business. If you do so, you would be worrying about the workload during your vacation, thereby losing out on the entire purpose behind the vacation. Plan it accordingly and relax.

Rewards

Having a proper reward system in place can be the biggest motivating factor to stick to your schedule and manage your time effectively. Often we tend to procrastinate because we believe that there is nothing rewarding about working. Would you still be interested to procrastinate if there was a lucrative reward waiting for you at the end of a day's hard work?

However, there are certain guidelines that need to be followed while setting up the reward system. If you have tall rewards, which are not justified by work, you will end up losing interest in the work and waste time, thereby making the reward system redundant. Let us look at some of the important rules that have to be borne in mind while determining the quantum of the rewards:

It should be worthy of the accomplishment

Your rewards should be justified by the amount of efforts and the work completed. If you reward yourself too much for a small accomplishment, the value of a reward is lost. On the other hand, if your rewards are negligible as compared to the amount of efforts that goes into every accomplishment, then you will not be motivated to work. Hence it is important that you strike a balance between your accomplishments and the reward system.

Be realistic

Do not promise to reward yourself something that is too expensive or something that is out of your reach. When you realize that you will not be able to afford it, you will feel dejected and lose interest in finishing your tasks within the predetermined time.

It should be immediate

Rewards should be timely. Only then, will it be capable of serving as a motivating factor. For instance, you have a project submission due this Friday. Promise to treat yourself over the weekend if you submit the project by Friday. This immediate rewarding system will motivate you to finish your goals for the next week with enthusiasm. You will realize that you will start managing your time in an efficient fashion, as there is a reward waiting for you at the end of the road for managing your time properly.

It should not be distracting

Make sure that the rewards that you promise yourself are not distracting in nature. Suppose you promise to reward yourself a new play station if you finish your project within the due date, understand that this could be detrimental especially if you are trying not to waste time. Hence choose a reward that will not be time consuming.

It should be healthy

If you wish to treat yourself to a nice dinner or lunch after accomplishing something, make sure it is something healthy. Falling sick could set you back by a lot and it will take some time for you to get back in track.

It should be positive and meaningful

Ensure that the rewards are positive and hold some meaning for you. Don't reward yourself something that you don't appreciate at all. The entire reward system will fail to achieve its purpose this way.

It should be specific

Do not have open ended rewards. For instance, you have an important meeting coming up and you have to work on a presentation. You could decide to go to a movie after finishing the presentation instead of just deciding to go out somewhere. Why is this important? When you have a specific reward in mind, it is easier to assess the time that goes hand in hand with the reward. In the above said example, if you just wish to go out somewhere, you will end up wasting a considerable amount of time in deciding where to go first and you will not have an idea upfront about the time requirements.

Managing Distractions

If you wish to use your time effectively, it is important that you find a way to deal with your distractions. Focus is important for you to achieve a given number of goals within the planned time.

Both external as well as internal factors play a major role when it comes to distractions. For instance, it could be as simple as the place where you have decided to work or study. If you decide to study in the park, you are bound to get distracted by the number of things that happen in the park. Let us look at the factors in detail.

External factors

As the name suggests, these distraction causing factors are based on the external environment you choose to work.

These factors are common to both students as well as those who are working.

✓ Noise:

Most of us cannot focus on work or studies if the place we choose to work is noisy. At this juncture, you are left with two options. If you are at the liberty to sit and study elsewhere, then find yourself a calm spot, preferably a library. On the other hand, if you have noisy colleagues and you don't have the luxury of shifting your workstation to some calm place in your office, get yourself an MP3 player and listen to calm and soothing music to zone out the external noise.

✓ Peer Pressure:

If you are a student, you will often have at least two friends in your gang who would not be interested to study. They would insist on spending the time on some leisure activities and taunt you till you agree to spend your time with them instead of studying. Learn to not succumb to such peer pressure. If you have a clear-cut schedule to follow, don't move away from it unless it is absolutely necessary.

Peers and other people can also come into play and influence your time management skills. For instance, co-workers, especially those not as busy as you are, can be a great source of distraction. That said, to become an effective time manager, you do not need to resign from your job; all you need is take necessary steps to avoid these distractions from idle co-workers.

How to Avoid Interruptions

Here is how to avoid distraction from peers (as well as how to avoid peer pressure)

To Avoid Casual Stop Bys' From Your Co-Workers, Close Your Door

If necessary, place a do not disturb sign on your door, and let people know that you should not be disturbed (unless there is an emergency) when your office door is closed.

Talk It Over

If someone in your workplace frequently disrupts you for non-essential matters, talk with the person about the problem. You may be surprised to learn that the person did not even realize he/she was distracting you.

Use Earphone or Headphones

If you work in an open office environment or a cubicle, you are less likely to see interruptions when wearing headphones, even if you are not listening to music.

✓ Visual distractions:

Many a times, most of us would rather spend our times gazing at the poster on our walls and daydreaming when we should have be utilizing the time for something effective. Remove such visual distractions and put them where you cannot see it. This will ensure that your attention is not divided.

Let us highlight some common visually distracting objects you probably did not consider risk to effective time management:

Common Visual Distractions and How to Avoid Them

The Internet

Despite being a good communication and access information tool, the internet can derail your productivity. Surfing the internet can take up a considerable amount of time. In fact, if you fail to exercise caution, when searching for one thing on the internet, a single minute can easily morph into thirty minutes or more. So is there a way to ensure you do not spend all your morning hours on the internet doing nothing productive?

How to Avoid

To avoid internet based distractions:

✓ Take short breaks to surf the internet. Small breaks after intensive work can be useful for resting your mind as they give you an opportunity to renew your energy.

✓ Keep your internet browser closed when you are not using it. However, some internet platforms such as Twitter can be a great source of news relative to your industry. Therefore, it is useful to check such a platform at specific times of the day.

✓ Read the news before you start your day: read newspapers or visit news websites before work to avoid distraction during the day. Ensure you allocate a specific time for this so that you do not get easily distracted.

✓ Use software applications such as anti-social or freedom to minimize online distractions. With these, you can specify websites you want to block and for how long.

✓ Block all distracting websites and apps: This happens to almost everyone. Let us assume an email notification comes in and you are tempted to check it out. In the process, every likelihood is that you will also be tempted to make a brief stopover on Twitter or other social media site and before you know it, 30 minutes are gone. There are applications and software that restrict specific website visit at specific times, use this to eliminate web distractions.

Instant Messaging

While instant messaging can be useful, many times, coworkers can use it as a way to interrupt you without having to get up from their workspaces. If you have to use instant messaging, make a point of using it for small and quick queries. However, if you still find it distracting, consider scheduling specific times for being online during the day. When you do not want instant messaging contact, set your status to "busy" or leave it off.

Phone, And Phone Calls

Having a state of the art Smartphone may cause addiction to playing games or surfing the net, which eventually, wastes precious time. Further, frequent phone calls from friends calling to wish you a good day can waste your time. Just because the phone is ringing does not necessarily mean you have to answer it especially when you are concentrating on something important. If possible, turn off your phone during your most productive working hours to minimize distractions. You could also inform your team that you will not be taking non-essential calls during specific times of the day.

Emails

Just like phone calls and instant messaging chats, frequent emails from subscribed services or advertisers can put a kink on your schedule. You need to manage the number and timing of received emails by following these steps:

How to Minimize Email Distractions

- ✓ Only check your email at specific times: Find the most appropriate time to check your email, and make it as infrequent as possible depending on the nature of your work. If you rely on email for business, you may want to check it regularly, maybe 3 times per day or so.

- ✓ Turn off audible email alerts: An alert every time someone sends you an email can waste a lot of time since your first instinct is to check what the email is about. This is allowing others to control your time. The only time you should check your email is when it is convenient or necessary to do so.

- ✓ Communicate in advance: In most cases, most of the queries you receive regularly through mail tend to be about the same issues. If you already have this information available to people in F.A.Q's on the intranet or your website, you can significantly reduce the queries you receive on a regular basis by communicating the existence of these files in advance

✓ Do not send emails in person: Avoid having to respond to emails in person unless otherwise stated; doing so can cause distraction and waste your time. Redirect any discussion that can be dealt with without having a debate over email. This will give you enough control over every query and the amount of time you give it. If email is not sufficient, use the phone. Otherwise, you can have a close confidant or employee attend to some of these mails.

✓ Physical clutter

Did you know that physical clutter could distract you from your work and alter your overall view of life? Unbelievable as it sounds, clutter can weigh you down, and eventually disrupt your effective time management skills.

For instance, working from a disorganized office or desk can be distracting. When your work life or workspace is in state of disorganization, you often find it difficult to think and plan effectively; hence, the importance of having an organized desk or home.

However, tackling clutter can sometime seem an uphill task, especially if you do not know where to start. Nevertheless, if you devote a little time to de-clutter your life, your will experience the pleasure of living in a relaxed environment, having a more organized and peaceful existence, as well as become a better time manager. Start to de-clutter your life, your home, and your work through a simplified, one-step at a time process outlined below.

Effective De-cluttering, Cleaning, and Organizing Tips for Time Managers

Let us see how you can effortlessly de-clutter your life:

De-Clutter the Office

Identify all the work you in your office, allocate ample space for each task or job, and then create a zone for each task, grouping relevant items accordingly. For instance, your work zone could include a desk and chair with a desktop, wastebasket, and printer, while your reference zone could accommodate your binders, shelves, and professional journals.

Before you can start de-cluttering your office, first de-clutter your cabinets, surfaces, drawers, and so on. Looking at the mountain of files spilling from your cabinets, it may seem like climbing Mt. Everest, but once you take the first bite, it gets a lot easier. Weed out the filing cabinets to make room for the several piles of office work on your desk. Next, clean out your inbox, coral your cord clutter, delete all the voice messages, and donate, or throw away anything you do not need or use.

Office Cleaning and De-Cluttering Tips

That said, the following tips prevent the accumulation of dust and thus make your cleaning faster:

✓ *Change Air Filters*
Make a habit of monitoring the condition of your air filters to ascertain if they are still working properly. Most air

filters have a lifespan of one and three months, but you should change them as soon as debris and dirt clogs them. Changing air filters will not only reduce dust in your office, but it will also extend the lifespan of your air conditioning system, making it easier to cool your office. You will also reduce your energy bill and achieve overall air quality.

Do Not Over-Polish

If you use a furniture polish or oil, avoid following the manufacturer's directions (manufactures want you to use their product, deplete it fast, and buy more). Overusing the product can cloud your wood surfaces, or cause a dust build up on furniture. A dry microfiber can come in handy because it picks up more dust and prevents the furniture from dust clouding or having a buildup of oily substances.

Repair Wood Surfaces

Take advantage of your pre-scheduled dusting time to repair any visible scratches on your wood furniture. A furniture crayon or marker can come in handy when going over the scratches during the dusting process. Use this time to remove adhesive stains, burn stains or candle wax from your furniture too.

Use Entrance Mats

To prevent the accumulation of dust, place two entrance mats at respective entrances, one outside the door and the other right inside. Be sure to select mats that are durable enough to withstand constant traffic in your office and remember to clean the mats regularly.

Clean and De-Clutter Your Living Room

Nothing cramps up a good evening as a living room cluttered mess after the guests have departed or when your kids have gone to bed. Fortunately, you can easily clean the mess in the living area in just a few minutes and still have a few leftover minutes. Cleaning and de-cluttering the living area can take a few minutes before going to work if you wake up early enough.

How to Clean and De-Clutter the Living Area

To clean and de-clutter the living area, follow these guidelines:

✓ Gather your supplies: Like with the previous rooms, this is one of the most important steps. Having your supplies ready before starting to clean means minimal distractions throughout the cleaning process.

✓ After collecting your basic supplies, the next step is to put all the items that should not be in the living room in a container. Since you are short on time (assuming you are doing it in the mornings) do not bother with placing items in their respective storage areas. Even without further distractions, you will waste time scurrying around the house multiple times placing each item in its rightful place.

✓ Organize the couch. Brush off the cushions and extract any items from underneath the couch. Remove the dirt from the interior of the couch and replace or fluff your pillows.

✓ Dust your coffee table and organize the contents well. Keep in mind that the point here is to brush off the table quickly and stack its contents neatly. Do not worry about making the furniture meticulously shine, or arranging the coffee table books alphabetically. Just neatly arrange the books and magazines

✓ Sweep or vacuum the floor. Do not move any furniture when doing this, or when vacuuming the couch and pillows. You can do these in a more detailed manner when you have more time. However, do not forget to take care of the dirt you brushed from the inside of the couch earlier on.

Keep aside your broom, vacuum or dust rag. Breathe and take a moment to enjoy your new living room.

Electronics

Save your shelf space by piling electronics over each other, but use plastic spacers to avoid overheating. Use wireless electronics when possible, and unbundle only the part of the cords from your electronics you are using in order to keep them out of the way.

Utilize Your Wall

Hang a bulletin board on your wall to organize the items you want to remember such as employee requests, post-its, and bills.

Paper Pushing

Establish a management system that will keep papers off your desk for documents. List all the types of documents you handle such as reports, bills and invoices, and find a storage space for each group.

The Small Things

Find a place within close reach to store loose items such as paper clips, pens, and stationary that you use often. It could be in a drawer or on your desk, but a multi compartment organizer will come in handy.

Internal Factors

These factors are subjective in nature. These can be overcome with few minor changes in our lifestyle and attitude.

✓ Physical distractions:

Irregular sleep patterns and lack of physical activity can have a direct impact on your attention span. When you don't sleep enough, you will have trouble concentrating while studying or working. Ensure that you get at least eight hours of sleep every day. Sufficient sleep is required to motivate the brain to work enough.

Getting enough sleep is helpful in that, when you are in a rested state, your brain internalizes information learnt throughout the day and then incorporates it into the long-term memory so that you can wake up fresh in the morning ready to learn new things.

Unfortunately, most of us tend to sacrifice sleep during a stressful or busy work schedule. The problem is that going without sleep in order to accomplish several tasks has a tendency to backfire on our faces. Even if you manage to complete all your tasks, your overall performance may not be impressive. Developing an effective time management schedule can solve this problem.

Hard as it may prove to be, getting enough sleep can help you become more productive. A goodnight sleep enhances your ability to manage time. On the other hand, without enough sleep, you increase your risk of stress. In simpler terms, lack of enough sleep cannot only reduce your performance it can also affect your overall health.

Time Management and Sleep: How to Get a Good Night Sleep

Since we have previously established the importance of enough sleep to time management, the following useful tips should ensure you get enough sleep every day:

Create a Good Sleep Environment

Excess light or heat can hinder sleep. Keep your bedroom dark, and use light blocking curtains if there is any disturbing source of light coming from the outside. In addition, ensure to keep your bedroom silent. In addition, make sure you keep all electronic devices such as computers and TVs away from your bedroom.

Change Your Workday Activities

Your workday can take a toll on your sleep patterns and affect your time management skills. Avoid heavy exercising right before bedtime, and stay away from any foods or beverages such as coffee, soda, tea, or chocolate containing caffeine late in the day. If you find it hard to sleep at night, minimize daytime naps to twenty minutes at most.

If you consume alcohol, do so in moderation. For instance, if you are a man, consume no more than two glasses of alcohol per day and if you are a woman, limit your intake to one glass of alcohol every day. In addition, if you smoke, attempt quitting because nicotine hinders sleep.

Develop a Routine

Go to bed and wake up at the same time every day. Also, avoid talking on the phone, eating, watching TV, or reading on an electronic device in bed. Avoid going to bed when stressed, and if you find yourself awake after twenty minutes in bed, get up, take a walk or do something relaxing, and then get back to sleep. If you think you have a sleeping problem, see a doctor.

Let us see some of the conditions that could warrant a doctor's appointment:

- ✓ Having a hard time staying awake during the day
- ✓ Difficulty waking up in the morning
- ✓ Loud and frequent snoring
- ✓ Pauses in breathing while sleeping

If you find yourself awake before your alarm clock sets off, then you are getting enough sleep. However, if you need your alarm clock to wake you up every day, consider adjusting your bedtime to an earlier time.

Take a Nap to Compensate For Lost Sleep

If you feel sleepy and need to make up for a few hours of lost sleep, take a daytime nap instead of sleeping late in order to compensate your sleep without altering your natural sleep wake cycle. Use the Nap Nap wheel to determine the best time to take a nap. Be smart about napping.

Taking a daytime nap is a powerful way to recharge, but it can also worsen insomnia. If you have insomnia, forget napping, and if you have to, do it early in the afternoon, and for not more than thirty minutes. Sleep experts agree that 10 to 20 minutes of a power nap is enough to refresh your mind, but depending on the purpose of your nap, other durations may be ideal as well.

If you want to boost your alertness, a 10 to 20 minute power nap will be enough to get you back to work shortly. On the other hand, to improve cognitive memory, you need a 60-minute nap, though a 90 minutes nap is ideally better. A ninety-minute nap will include a full sleep cycle; this type of nap will improve creativity as well as procedural and emotional memory. In addition to this, experts suggest sitting slightly upright when taking your nap because apparently, doing so helps you avoid deep slumber. If you dream during naps, it could be a sign of sleep deprivation.

Fight After-Dinner Drowsiness
This is a normal thing to experience. If you feel sleepy way before your regular bedtime, stand up and do something stimulating to avoid falling asleep, say calling a friend, washing the dishes, or getting your clothes ready for the following day. If you sleep earlier than your regular bedtime, you might wake up in the middle of the night and experience difficulty falling back to sleep.

✓ *Self Talk:*
Most of us have the habit of talking to ourselves in an attempt to motivate ourselves. But sometimes we go overboard and end up talking to ourselves more than what

is necessary. Allocate a certain amount of time for self talk and ensure that you don't end up wasting a lot of time talking to yourself.

✓ *Personal issues:*

Most of us have personal issues that we have to deal with. Often we end up worrying about these issues while working or studying. Sometimes, it might be difficult to take these things off our mind. But if the work is important or if you have an important test coming up, you cannot afford to not prepare for it. You might have to figure out a way to empty your mind and focus on the tasks to be completed.

Other Ways to Eliminate Distractions

Do you want to get more done in less time? Eliminating distractions will help you accomplish more. In addition to everything we have previously outlined, the following guidelines will help you eliminate distractions and ensure that you accomplish more tasks.

1. Breakdown Tasks

It is easy to get distracted when the task at head seems difficult to accomplish; tasks that seem bigger at first glance might even cause you to procrastinate. Huge tasks become easier to accomplish when broken down into easier smaller ones that when combined, ensure the completion of the big task. Research has also found that it is easier to become, and remain motivated to accomplish smaller tasks than it is to get motivation for larger tasks.

2. Track Your Time Expenditure

Either way you look at it, distractions come in many forms. To remove distractions from your daily routine, you must track how your time expenditure because doing so will help you learn which tasks attract a lot of self-distraction. A handy tools tool you can use is a time tracker app that you can install on your smart phone. As you track your time, try to create a schedule for this. A schedule is very essential in helping you manage time. It is also effective in limiting distraction. If you set a schedule, it indicates that you intend to follow it; this makes it harder to get distracted.

3. Train Your Brain to Focus

Did you know that your brain is still the biggest distraction you can ever have? If your brain is jumping from one topic to the other on subjects unrelated to what you are aiming to accomplish, you cannot stay focused. You can train your mind by learning how to control it.

In most instances, training the mind is just as simple as paying attention to your own attention and stopping impulses before they take root in the brain. Meditation effectively trains you mind to concentrate on specific aspects at a given time.

4. Say No to Stress

Work related stress is a hindrance to effective time management and productivity. To boost performance, you need to identify factors that cause stress and deal with them effectively.

How to Say No to Stress: 5 Easy Tips

To say no stress, here are effective, and easy to adopt tips:

1. Understand Stress

Stress is a normal physical and psychological reaction to the never-ending demands of life. Studies have shown that most of us experience challenges in dealing with stress at some point in the year.

Some situations that cause stress and consume the limited time you have are not impossible to solve. Learn to look for a remedy to your problems so that you can feel in control and save time. If unsure of how to begin, write down the problem and then brainstorm many possible solutions, then pick each solution and analyze the good and bad side of it to realize a safe and reliable solution. Highlight each step you must undertake to solve the problem, i.e. what to do, how to do it, when to complete and who to be involved.

When considering the root causes of your stress, and your response to it, these two steps can help:

1. Identify Your Stressors

Most of your day is rich in activities, tasks, and obligations. However, can you tell which of these activities, tasks, and obligations inflame stress? To detect stressors, keep a log and record the situations that create the most stress in your job or family life. Record your thoughts and feelings, as well as information describing your work environment, the people and situations involved, and your actions. Be aware that eating a wheat-processed snack from the vending machine could also cause stress.

2. Develop Healthy Responses

Once you are gain familiarity with causes of stress, find healthy choices to respond to stress, rather than turning to alcohol or fast food. A good way to deal with stress is through exercise such as yoga. You can also incorporate favorite fun activities and hobbies in your schedule. These could be going to concerts, reading a book, or playing games with family.

On the other hand, taking time to recharge can ease stress. Research has shown that replenishing your energy in whichever way can prevent the effects of chronic stress and burnout. Replenishing your energies may mean completely disconnecting from work related activities from time to time, without even thinking about work during this time. Vacations are a great way to relax and unwind, so take advantage of these in order to come back to work feeling rejuvenated.

3. Learn To Relax

Techniques you can use to melt away stress include deep breathing exercises, meditation, and mindfulness, a state where you actively observe current experiences without judging them. Spend a few minutes every day focusing on a simple activity such as enjoying a meal, walking, or breathing.

In the technology driven world we inhabit, relaxation does not come as easy as it should. That said, here are a few ways to relax and reduce every day stress.

2. Create Boundaries

Technology today has made it possible for us to be available 24 hours a day. However, you need to establish a balance between work and personal life. Avoid reading your work emails or answering work-related phone calls at home to prevent a potential work life conflict that often births unmanageable stress.

3. Talk to Your Boss

Though not always so, chances are, your boss desires to create a favorable work environment. Start by having an open discussion with your supervisor, not just to lay down a list of complaints, but also to come up with an effective strategy for managing the identified stressors.

4. Get Support

One effective way to manage stress is seeking, and accepting help from your support network, including your friends and family. Some companies even have available stress management resources through an employee assistance program. However, if any of these and the previous methods does not work for you, you may want to see a psychologist to help you manage your stress through therapy.

On the other hand, going to work when refreshed or well rested is vital to having a productive day. These simple steps can facilitate you overcome these embarrassing issues:

5. Watch your diet: the food you eat affects your level of tiredness. Avoid heavy lunches and eat smaller, healthy snacks past afternoon.

6. Stay hydrated: when dehydrated, for lack of drinking enough water, you may not think clearly.

7. Go for a walk: if exhaustion assaults you while at work, get up and go for a walk. Physically moving your body and getting some fresh air can give you more energy and keep you alert.

8. Massage Your Head

There is no better way to relieve stress immediately than with a head massage. Effective head massage techniques essentially involve a blend of different pressure points as well as appropriate strokes and positioning. Apart from helping you relieve stress, a good head massage can go a long way in providing relief from chronic headaches, and a good night's sleep. A good approach is to use herbal or natural oils such as avocado oil, neem oil and olive oil, which contain beneficial nutrients when administering the massage.

A Good Head Massage Procedure

- ✓ Spread your fingers on the head, and then stroke it gently in an upward and downward motion.

- ✓ Exert pressure on the head with the fingertips only. Be sure to change the motion of the fingers every couple of minutes.

- ✓ Change the movement of your fingers to a clockwise and anticlockwise direction. To feel relaxed, be sure to apply pressure to the back and side of your head using the knuckles on the inside of your hand.

- ✓ Pull the top of your ears with your fingers until you hear a sort of cracking sound. This helps reduce tension as well as in expanding the muscles of the ear.

✓ Apply pressure on your eyebrows using your thumb and index finger only for instant headache relief.

✓ Conclude the head massage by closing your eyes and then massage your sockets very gently using your index finger only.

Some benefits you can derive from an effective head massage include providing relief from insomnia, fatigue, sinusitis, stress, migraines as well as increasing your mental clarity, hair thinning, and scalp tension.

9. Breathe

When stress hits, it is a usual thing for your breathing to rise. Your breathing also tends to be shallower and from the chest. A deep breathing exercise should allow you take fuller and slower breaths that reflect your true relaxed state. Deep breathing helps you counter stress by slowing your heart rate and reducing blood pressure.

To enhance both the physical and mental wellbeing and to keep chronic stress at bay, practice this 3-minute breathing exercise at any time. The breathing exercise can help you decrease feelings of anger, frustration, or tension.

An Effective 3-Minute Breathing Exercise

✓ Sit comfortably in an upright posture

✓ Pay attention to your current state and existence, and block any intrusive thoughts that creep up. Keep your eyes tightly closed to eliminate external stimuli.

✓ Now concentrate on your breathe. Start inhaling through the nose, a take a few seconds.

✓ Exhale through the mouth, and attempt to make the exhalation last 2 times longer than the inhalation.

✓ Progress with this breathing technique for 3-5 minutes; If you enjoy the alertness and relieved state of mind, increase the practice session to around 15-20 minutes daily.

To achieve relaxation in stressful conditions exercise regularly.

10. Exercise

Exercising is essentially meant to build muscles and enhance physical fitness. However, exercise does more than tone the muscles; it also plays a major role in building your brain. Exercise has the ability to improve mood, avert the symptoms of depression, and enhance healthy aging of the brain, overcome dementia and memory loss. In addition, recent studies have shown that exercise improves mental focus and cognitive performance, which effectively helps you deal with any challenges throughout your day. Exercise can help reduce stress, help you effectively manage your time, as well as increase your brainpower.

To exercise, you do not have to go overboard; all you have to do is choose a few activities you enjoy, by following these quick tips:

Exercise and Effective Time Management: Exercise Tips

Pick up a new hobby or sport to improve learning: Getting a new hobby or sport that requires fancy foot moves, or hand eye coordination can enhance growth of new brain cells. In addition, taking up complicated activities can also improve your concentration skills in the short run.

Try mild daily workouts to retain memory: A scientific study found out that the elderly who engage in leisure activities such as gardening, cooking, short walks, and cleaning have a lower risk of developing a crumbling vocabulary and memory loss. This research proves that exercise plays a role in boosting short term or long term memory.

Undertake Steady Activities: Research shows that if you burn around 350 calories thrice a week through consistent and moderate activity, you can significantly reduce symptoms of depression. In addition, exercise can work as a compliment to therapy and medications to help control depression. Stress, anxiety, and depression are hindrance to effective performance at work; exercising is almost as effectively as using antidepressants.

Use Cardio To Enhance Immediate Mental Performance: Cardio exercises fight stress and relax a troubled mind. A short and sweaty session of running, jumping rope, and squat bends quickly improves blood flow to your brain. Incorporate mini cardio workouts to your work schedule at least one hour before you start working.

Dance: Stress and fatigue affect your mood and slow you down. Getting 'Jiggy with it' is one way to relief tense muscles and fight stress; dancing gets the body moving and curbs muscular pains and aches. When you dance, the heart pumps blood into the vessels and your heart starts racing. Further, the body releases hormones and endorphins, thus, you feel energized and happy. A light dance, especially when accompanied with some fast-paced music to make it a joyous experience should help you experience fun and forget all the stress and anxiety.

Though all dances can greatly relief stress, fast-paced dances among them tango, hip-hop, swing, and salsa are the best. If you have a partner, attend a dancing class and engage in the dance as a joint activity. To begin dancing:

- ✓ Start slow, get a few songs you enjoy; or songs that can let you follow the tempo.

- ✓ Be in a comfortable outfit that allows you to bend or sway the muscle easily. Look for ample space free from obstruction

- ✓ If possible, dim the lights and shelf all problems you have. Only pay attention to the music, think 'calm', and cleanse your thoughts.

- ✓ Stretch your arms using slow bending poses to relief stress, as you move slowly to the music.

- ✓ Take a number of deep breaths, smile, and shelf all worries; maintain balance, and move in time to your music.

- ✓ Then change to fast-paced music. Shift to a strong, loud and refreshing music and dance to it as if your life depends on it! Allow all stress, anger, and anxiety to escape until you feel energized. By now, your focus should be on the dancing, not the problems.

- ✓ Gradually slow down to feel calm and avoid exhaustion; once relaxed, consume a healthy drink or some water and continue listening to soft music.

✓ Create a playlist that consists of nature sounds such as birds chirping, bubbling brook, or the ocean. Then let the mind focus onto the variety of instruments, melodies, or singers in one piece.

Alternatively, you can blow off some steam by simply rocking out to upbeat tunes, or even singing at the top of the lungs.

11. Think and Visualize

Thinking and visualization are very effective stress management techniques. To get started on their implementation:

Think Positively

Negative thinking is one of the most toxic elements that can hinder you from making positive changes in life. Negative thoughts can slow your mind and prevent you from advancing your career and personal life.

Whether you are aware of it or not, your brain keeps on thinking, and if you allocate time to monitoring your thoughts, it will surprise you to learn just how negative you can be. That said; how can you stop yourself from negative thinking?

How to Stop Negative Thinking and Think Positively

These tips can help you become an effortless positive thinker.

Monitor Your Thoughts

It does not matter if you take ten minutes or an hour: it is not possible to fix something you are not aware of. By observing your thoughts, you will get an idea of where to start.

Change the Negative Thoughts

Everyone has that one thought that dominates his or her mind. Whatever it is, take that main agenda and transform it into an affirmation. Rather than concentrating on the extra weight you have, just say to yourself, "I am beautiful exactly the way I am". While this will obviously not make you lose weight instantly, it will go a long way in giving you confidence and inspiration.

Select a Mantra of the Day

Determine a daily mantra in the morning and repeat it slowly to yourself as you go about your day. It could be something simple such as "I am a happy person" or "Today is a beautiful day". Using a mantra will go a long way in giving you something positive to think about and keep your brain from wondering to negative thoughts.

Establish a Gratitude List

When you are feeling down and off, take time to come up with a list of 3-5 things you are grateful for and put them down on paper. Even simple things such as reading a good book or owning a functional car are great things to be thankful for. The best thing about a gratitude list is that it can change your mood and bring your focus back to the positive things in life.

Use an App

Modern life is technology driven, and there is an app for almost everything, even positive thinking. One such great app is the Stress free life.

Visualize

If used well, creative visualization can help you develop a clear vision of what you want to achieve. A good way to make the most of your visualization is to create a strategy. When it comes to visualization, it is not advisable to concentrate on the results; but rather use this technique once you are done with the groundwork. For instance, an amateur player or attaché at a job would be required to focus on the basics as compared to professionals who can actually visualize a possible dream. When you have determined the necessary steps, it becomes much easier to visualize yourself finishing them.

It's advisable to concentrate on actionable tasks as this can bring benefits among them:

- ✓ Reinforcing positive behavior
- ✓ Eliminating self-defeating thoughts
- ✓ Overcoming procrastination

Through visualization, it is possible to cultivate healthy habits that help you achieve your goals. Among the most important factors that may go a long way in establishing new habits and positive behaviors is the act of repetition. The best thing about visualization is that you can concentrate on building these new patterns without the fear of failure.

Every time you try something new, there is always the probability that you will not succeed with the first attempt.

However, visualization enables you to make several attempts and find the best approach before you even try it in the real world. Visualization even allows you to correct errors during visualization before overcoming them in the real world. You can get anywhere you want if you apply the appropriate creative visualization techniques.

Meditate

Meditating on everyday can alter your brain's neural pathways, and thus make you resilient to stress. Meditating means undergoing a mental exercise where you focus on your breathing or repeat a mantra. Various meditation practices quiet your mind and relief stress and anxiety. You do not have to do complicated stuff to meditate properly.

A Simple Meditation Exercise

- ✓ Begin by sitting up straight with your feet on the floor, and closed eyes

- ✓ Concentrate on reciting a positive mantra such as "I love myself" or "I feel God" either silently or loudly.

- ✓ Put one hand on your belly to synchronize the mantra with your breathing.

- ✓ Allow distracting and anxious thoughts to float away like clouds in the sky.

Consume a Mood Boosting Diet

Simply put, the foods you eat directly affect your mood or feelings; thus, watch what you put on your plate. Aim for a healthy and balanced diet rich in low fat proteins, complex carbohydrates, as well as fruits and vegetables. On the other hand, minimize foods that have an adverse impact on your brain and mood, including caffeine, Trans-fats, alcohol, foods rich in chemical preservatives and saturated fats.

A Few Diet Ideas to Get You Started

Here are a few diet ideas to start you off:

- ✓ *Do Not Skip Meals*: Skipping meals can make you feel tired and irritable. Therefore, eat something light every 3 to 4 hours.

- ✓ *Limit Your Refined Carbs And Sugar Intake*: While depression can make you crave for baked goods, sugary snacks, or comfort foods such as French fries or pasta, these foods can lead to a drop in energy and mood.

- ✓ *Concentrate on Complex Carbohydrates*: Complex carbs include baked potatoes, oatmeal, whole-wheat pasta, and whole grain breads. These can boost your level of serotonin without causing a crush in mood.

- ✓ *Improve Your B Vitamins*: A deficiency of group B vitamins like Vitamin B12 and folic acid is a recipe for depression. To get more, eat more eggs, chicken, beans, leafy greens, and citrus fruit, or take a vitamin B complex vitamin supplement.

- ✓ *Eat Super Foods*: Super foods with high levels of nutrients can improve your mood. Bananas in particular have magnesium that decreases anxiety, while brown rice has thiamine and serotonin that support sociability. Spinach is also rich in magnesium and folate that improve sleep and reduces agitation.

✓ *Try A Chromium Supplement*: Chromium picolinate eases mood swings, reduces carbohydrate cravings, and boosts energy. This may come in handy especially if you have a tendency to eat too much and oversleep when depressed.

Chapter 6: Tips for Effective Time Management

We had highlighted the broad ways to manage your time in the previous chapter. In this chapter, let us look at some tips which when incorporated in your everyday life can help you with effective time management.

Tips:

We might have covered some of these in the previous chapter. Nevertheless, you can use these tips as quick reference tools.

✓ Have your schedule printed and keep it with you. You could keep a diary with you. Keep recording any deviations from the schedule in it. At the end of the day, you will be able to assess how effectively your day was spent in meeting the goals for the day.

✓ Make sure you assign time for any activity. It can be as trivial as a phone call or as important as a meeting. When you assign time for it, you will make a conscious effort to keep your conversations precise and crisp.

✓ Allocate some time for thinking as well as planning the modalities of execution of certain tasks. Sometimes, you need to take a break and analyze the task on hand.

✓ Always take into consideration the different distractions and interruptions that might come your way. When you take cognizance of these disruptions, you will be able to plan your time accordingly.

✓ Spend the first thirty minutes of your day to plan your day out. We often think that planning is a waste of time. On the contrary, planning your day helps you in assessing the different tasks on hand and allot time for each task on hand. This way, you will end up saving a lot of time, which you might have wasted on irrelevant stuff in the absence of a plan.

✓ Before you make an important business call, take five minutes to go over the purpose of the call. Understand the importance of the call and analyze the various outcomes of the call. This will help you in steering the conversation in the most effective way and help you achieve the desired results in a time effective manner.

✓ If required, learn to put a "Do not disturb" sign outside your study room or workstation if you are working on something important and cannot afford to get distracted. As mentioned earlier, it is important that you learn to deal with distractions. Often, we are disturbed and interrupted in the middle of work by others. Since it is not possible for us to ask them to leave the room without offending them all the time, an easy way to keep such distractions at bay would be to put a sign outside your door before you begin any important work.

✓ Keep a track of your progress. Keep reviewing how much you have completed at regular intervals. When you assess your progress regularly, you will be able to take stock of the work left to be completed.

✓ Do one thing at a time. Don't try answering an email when you are on a call. You will end up wasting more time to fix the errors that arise out of multi-tasking.

✓ Learn to delegate. It is not necessary that you have to do everything yourself. If you can delegate some of your tasks to someone else and get it done, then do not shy away from doing it. Delegation will not only save your time but also help you in getting multiple things done at the same time.

✓ Keep a clock nearby to be always aware of the time. This is because we often end up getting immersed in our work and not keep a tab on time. What happens when we get too engrossed in our work is that we end up spending more time than what is required to complete the task. However, when you have a clock in front of you, you will consciously be aware of the time you are spending on the current task and you will be able to take necessary steps if you are running short of time.

✓ Do not waste time focusing on trivial details that do not matter. Often, we get distracted by these unimportant things that are not important in the larger scheme of things and end up wasting a lot of time on them. Refrain from doing so and you will realize how much time you have in hand to focus on important things.

✓ Make use of tools like reminders, organizers, and alarms to keep track of your time. We cannot solely rely on the recalling capacity of our brain to remind us about upcoming meetings or exams or birthdays. Hence, there is no harm in making use of these tools to keep a tab on things as it is not humanely possible to remember everything unless we have photographic memory.

✓ Learn to say no. We tend to take up more than what we can chew and this is why we are submerged in deadlines often. Take up only work that you are very sure of delivering within the stipulated timeline. Do not over-commit and kill yourself in the process. It is absolutely professional to turn down work instead of over-committing and failing to deliver.

✓ Sleep at least for seven to eight hours in a day. We are often led to believe that sleep is considered as a waste of time. This is perhaps the reason why most of us tend to work for long hours by staying up. We think that our productivity will be enhanced by sleeping less and working more. However, this trick will not work in the long run. For your body and mind to function normally without any issues, it is important that you sleep for at least for seven to eight hours a day. This optimal sleep is required to ensure the proper functioning of your body. A healthy body and mind is required if you wish to increase your productivity. Moreover, you will be able to get more work done in less time when you are healthy.

✓ Convert the key tasks into your daily habits. For instance, if you are a student, you will have to prepare for your classes or exams. Instead of studying in the last minute, make studying a habit. Allot time for studying every day and follow it. It will eventually become a habit. This way, your efficiency will be improved tremendously.

✓ Allow for some buffer time between two tasks. Though it may look good on paper to list out all the tasks to be completed and allot time without a break, it is not practical for us to follow the list. This is because; we might take a short break after each task. Or we might have other things lined up. For instance, you are working on a project report and you receive a phone call. However, you decide to handle the phone call after finishing the task on hand i.e. the project report. Hence once you are done with the report, you will not immediately begin to work on the next item in your to-do list. Instead, you would proceed to make this phone call. Hence it is important that we plan for these breaks ahead and include the buffer time in our plan as well.

✓ Do not get overwhelmed easily. Sometimes, we tend to get overwhelmed by looking at our to-do list. This can discourage us from working. Instead of looking at the number of tasks to be completed for the day, focus on one task at a time. This way, you will see for yourself that your to-do list was completely doable by the end of the day.

✓ Do not let go of weekends. Yes, weekends are the time allotted for leisure and rest. But if you go the extra mile and get a fraction of your work done during the weekend, you will see yourself handling the forthcoming week with ease. For instance, if you have a 3000 words essay due by Wednesday, you can start working on it from Saturday and finish a portion of it, say 500 words. This way, you will be able to submit the essay by Tuesday, which is well within the due date. This gives you time to focus on the other important tasks lined up for Wednesday.

✓ Often, we spend a lot of time travelling or waiting. Try to utilize this time as well. For instance, instead of sitting idle inside the metro, you can get some studying done or prepare for your upcoming presentation at work. Carry a book or your laptop with you always. If that is not possible, at least carry your diary with you. You can use the time spent in waiting rooms or inside the cab to plan for the reminder of the day and the next day.

✓ Group all related activities together. This way, you will be able to save a lot of time. For instance, all the errands that require you to travel can be clubbed together. This way, you will not only save your time but also the fuel. Similarly, you can club all your business calls together and take them during a certain time. This way, you will not be disturbed during the rest of the day.

✓ Find some time to absolutely stay still. Though this might sound like a time wasting endeavor, this can actually help in improving your focus tremendously. Try not to do anything during this time and stay absolutely still. This silence can reduce your anxiety and take care of your stress levels. Ideally by the end of this exercise, you would be rejuvenated mentally to take up the next tasks with more enthusiasm and lesser anxiety.

✓ Learn to have fun. All work and no play will sap out the motivation and energy in you. Learn to make time for your leisure activities as well. It is highly important that you have some work life balance. Work life balance is important to keep you motivated as well as focused. Hence ensure that you don't compromise on your leisure activities just because you are tied up with work.

✓ Maintain a time log. List out all the tasks that need to be completed for the day. List out the time assigned for each task next. As and when you begin working on a task, record the start time against the task. When you complete the task, note down the end time. This will show you how much time you actually took to finish the task. This will also help you assess how your time estimate for finishing the task actually matches with the time taken to finish it.

✓ Maintain a positive attitude. It is important to stay optimistic and confident before you begin any task. If you fail to have a positive attitude, your motivation to work will be drastically affected. This in turn will affect your productivity. In other words, you will end up spending a lot of time to get the job done if you don't possess the right mindset to work. Hence it is highly important to have the right mindset before you begin your day.

✓ Learn to persevere. Sometimes, it is not possible for us to complete what we had aimed to complete for the day. As mentioned earlier, there are certain distractions that cannot be avoided completely. These distractions will end up eating up our time leaving us with less time to finish the tasks on hand. The common reaction to such a situation would be to sulk and give up. However, what is needed at this juncture is the ability to persevere. Do not give up even if there are certain unwarranted delays. Keeping working hard towards the achievement of your goals.

✓ Learn to be early on time. Most often, we plan to complete the tasks assigned to us on time. This way, we end up completing the tasks either on time or after the stipulated time. To avoid missing deadlines, plan to finish your tasks well before the time. This way, even if there are unforeseen distractions, you will be able to finish the task either early or on time. This is a sure way to ensure that you do not miss out on deadlines.

✓ Set reminders at least fifteen minutes before the meeting. Most reminder apps come with this feature. This way, you will be prepared for the meeting at least fifteen minutes before the scheduled time. In case your meeting is scheduled at an off campus venue, then keep a reminder at least an hour early for you to plan your travel to the venue accordingly.

Chapter 7: Mistakes to Avoid

Now that you have a detailed overview of the process of time management, let us go over the common mistakes that are associated with time management. Most of these mistakes have already been highlighted in the earlier sections of this book. However, I have reiterated the common mistakes to avoid to ensure that you manage your time effectively. I have briefly gone over these mistakes as most of them have already been dealt with in detail in the previous chapters of this book.

1. **Failing to keep a To-do list:**

This is the most common mistake everyone tends to commit. We think that we have got it all captured inside our minds and fail to maintain a to-do list. There are several apps available these days that can facilitate the recording of the tasks to be done for the day if you think you do not have the time of preparing the To-do list the conventional way using a paper and a pen.

Apart from To-do lists, you can also adopt other 3 major types of lists:

- My schedule, which comprises of activities you intend engage in for an entire year
- People-to-Call List; here you have a list of the most important calls to make within a stipulated period, organized alphabetically
- Conference Planner: in your Conference planner, have a page for every person you interact with; simply write down the issues you want to talk to them about in conversations or meetings.

The rule of the thumb is to prepare a regimented, regularly used list-making system to work for you. Research shows business people who fail to make use of lists are probably not making much money either.

2. Failing to prioritize

Most people come up with a To-do list but do not know how to prioritize the tasks. The importance of prioritizing your tasks has already been stressed enough in the previous sections of this book. Failing to do so will end up wasting a lot of your time.

3. Failing to track your time

It is highly important that you understand the value of your time. The value of our time can be understood only when we keep track of it. We will be able to identify those redundant areas where our time is being wasted when we keep a track on our time. When we don't track our time, you can be sure that it is not being used in the most effective manner.

4. Procrastinating

Procrastinating is nothing but putting off the tasks to be completed to a future time. This is the biggest mistake when it comes to time management. We not only fail to follow our schedule when we procrastinate but also eat up time allotted for the other tasks by doing the postponed task at that time. Procrastination can have a toll on your efficiency too if it becomes a habit. Most people end up chasing deadlines because they are constantly procrastinating.

On the other hand, procrastination only makes you end up spending a lot of time later on doing the task that you could have simply done within a shorter time. For instance, if you keep postponing washing every utensil you use to the end of the week, you will find that by Saturday, you have many dishes to wash; the dishes would require a longer time to clean because the dirt and grease may have stuck to the utensils, which also demands for more effort to wash. However, if you had simply decided to wash the dishes after a meal, every day, you would only spend a few minutes doing the task without much effort.

That said; the few steps below can help you overcome procrastination and effectively manage your time (we have previously touched on how to overcome procrastination- this is merely adding to what we outlined earlier)

Acknowledge That You Are Procrastinating

One of the most honest ways to prove that you procrastinate tasks is to judge yourself with a lot of honesty. To help you do that; you can use these unbiased indicators of procrastination:

- ✓ Have low priority tasks at the top of your to do list

- ✓ Waiting for the right time or the right mood to carry out an important task

- ✓ Postponing a task on your To-do list for a prolonged time, even when you are aware that it is important

- ✓ Revisiting emails several times without taking action on them

- ✓ Sitting down to start an urgent task but almost immediately taking off to get some coffee

✓ Difficulty saying no to other people's unimportant tasks, rather than using the time to get done with relevant, important tasks

Evaluate What Makes You Procrastinate

Doing this is important because causes of procrastinating can be internal or external. For instance, you may find a particular job to be unpleasant, and as such, will try to avoid it for that reason. The quandary is that most jobs have a boring or unpleasant aspect, and the best way to deal with these is to do them quickly and get them over with, so that you can concentrate on the more pleasant aspects of the job.

On the other hand, you could be disorganized, and therefore find it hard beating procrastination. However, if you have a prioritized schedule and To-do-list, you will know the relevance of the task, and can even calculate the time it will take to complete it, then work back from that point to avoid late deadlines.

If you are an organized person but feel overwhelmed by a task, you may doubt the skills and resources needed to complete the assignment, so you end up doing the things you are sure of. Perfectionists are surprisingly often procrastinators, who often negate completing a task for fear of their inability to do the task perfectly right away. Furthermore, poor decision making skills can cause procrastination. If you cannot decide what you want to do, then you are more likely to avoid taking action in case anything goes wrong.

Adopt Anti-Procrastination Techniques

Since procrastination is a weakness or a deeply ingrained habit, it is not possible to break it overnight. You will need to work on this bad habit day after day. Here are some general tips to get you moving:

✓ Set Rewards: For instance, promise yourself a piece of chocolate cake or your favorite steaks if you complete a certain task by lunchtime.

✓ Ask a Pal to check up on you: fellow employees or friends who you share the same job category can help you do this. Self-help groups use this technique, and it is widely recognized as a very effective approach.

✓ Determine and acknowledge the unpleasant consequences of not finishing the task: For instance, failure to accomplish business tasks within stipulated deadlines could cost you a business deal or entire professional career.

✓ Evaluate The Cost Of Your Time To Your Employers: Your employers are paying you to work on tasks they think are most relevant. If you are not doing these things, you are not delivering value for your earnings.

✓ Maintain a To-do-list: A To-do list will help you avoid overwhelming or unpleasant tasks slipping off your mind. If you simply fail to follow your To-do-list due to a busy working schedule, try setting up a reminder on your smart phone, or have a close friend help you follow your self-laid plan.

✓ Become a master of project planning and scheduling in order to know when to start all-important projects.

✓ Set Time Limits for Your Goals: Set time limits even for less urgent tasks. Doing this can help you stop wasting time and let you save time for impromptu demands.

✓ If A Task or Project Seems Too Overwhelming, break it into smaller, manageable bits that are easy to accomplish within a stipulated time.

✓ Do Not Be Selective On Tasks: If you are avoiding a task because you think it unpleasant, try it. It may turn out to be the opposite of what you were expecting.

5. Multitasking and How It Affects Time Management

The rule of the thumb is to concentrate on one task at a time. Although multitasking can at times be productive, avoid straining yourself with multiple tasks as each of them may require full attention.

Actually, engaging in a single task at a time can bring more benefits compared to multitasking. For instance, when you concentrate on one task, you boost your productivity. If you focus on one task before moving on to the other, you give one task your divided attention. This is especially helpful in work projects that require perfectionism. No one can deny that giving your attention to one task also translates into productivity.

Dealing with a single task helps you become an effective time manager. Regardless of how hardworking you believe you are, it is difficult to perform two tasks in the same or lesser time. Multitasking consumes more time and is counterproductive.

How Multitasking Affects You

Let's see some reasons why multitasking could be costing you.

Less Concentration

It is almost impossible to give two or more tasks your full attention without causing a conflict. A study by Stanford University revealed that people exposed to multiple streams of electronic information did not pay attention compared to those who did not multitask. On the contrary, those who opted to watch one stream of digital data before moving on to other streams were more in control of their memory. Juggling tasks will create an urgency that never goes away.

May Cause Attention Deficit Disorder

Did you know that exposure to email and other technological multitasking habits can temporarily lower your IQ by 10 points? This is not a joke as concluded by findings from a study conducted by Kings College in London. Multitasking strongly links to attention deficit disorder (ADD). Actually, medical officers compare multitasking to playing tennis using two balls. Their point of view is that constant jumps between tasks leads to reduced performance and productivity and inflames the symptoms of ADD.

Increases Downtime

Multitasking also increases downtime in workers because, when you leave a task and move on to another task, it is very hard to carry on the previous task form where you left off. Due to streams of work competing for your attention when you are multitasking, it becomes extremely difficult to focus.

Too many breaks

Just like how not taking enough breaks is harmful when it comes to your productivity, taking too many breaks is also equally dangerous. Often, when we find the task in hand tedious, we tend to take small breaks to not let the difficulty affect us. What happens when we don't keep a tab on these breaks is that we might end up taking too many of them and waste time. Hence ensure that your breaks are consistent and are for a short duration. Your break time should not end up being more than your work time.

Bearing the burden

It has become so common to come off as a hard worker by taking too much burden at work. Most of the times, this burden is highly unnecessary and unwarranted for. Most of us tend to forget that success at workplace is all about smart work and not hard work. An easy way to ensure that you don't take up unnecessary burden at work is to delegate. Delegate those tasks, which can be done by the others in your team as well. This way, you can focus better on those tasks that require your full attention.

Planning too much

Yes, it is important that you plan for your day. But most of us get carried away with the entire process of planning. We end up spending a lot of time on planning instead of focusing on the execution of the tasks. Know what the maximum time is you can afford to spend on planning. Ensure that you do not overstep this time limit and plan too much.

Not planning enough

Just like how planning too much is bad, not planning enough is also bad. When you don't plan enough, it reflects your attitude towards work. Every aspect of our day needs to be planned well in advance. Of course, there will be deviations and unwarranted distractions. But you should plan for them nevertheless. When you don't plan properly, you don't really take into consideration the actual aspects of the task and allot a proper time for it. You end up allocating a rough estimate for each task which may be far-fetched. To avoid these discrepancies, plan enough.

Being busy

Keeping yourself busy all the time is not a sign of your efficiency. On the contrary, when you are perpetually busy, it means that you are doing a lot of non-essential things just to keep you occupied. When we keep ourselves engaged in less important tasks, we hardly have time to focus on the more important things that require our attention. Moreover, when you are always busy, you end up being under a lot of stress constantly. Understand where your time is getting spent mostly and assess if it is worth the time spent. This will help you in handling your time well. In fact, most successful people are seldom perpetually busy. This is perhaps why they find time for things other than work as well such as vacations, social gatherings etc.

6. Running Meetings

Meetings are one of the best communication and management tools, thus, there is need to learn proper meeting strategies to save time, solve problems, boost production, and increase motivation. Meetings work because written word only carries about 7 percent of the true feeling or understandable meaning.

Meetings are more effective compared to telephone conversation, which only offer 38 percent of the true meaning and feelings in the manner things are communicated. During an actual meting, 55 percent of the feelings or true meanings are carried by non-verbal signals such as facial expression.

Why Hold Meetings: Benefits

Here are few benefits of holding meetings:

✓ Meetings create new ideas and initiatives.

✓ They help solve conflicts in a way that emails and memos cannot.

✓ Meetings achieve buy-in.

✓ Meetings prevent 'not invented here' syndrome.

For effective meetings, the rule of the thumb is to plan, hold, and follow-up meetings in the correct manner, to help repay the cost involved in the facilitation of face-to-face interaction. Meetings can help you manage teams and events, achieve your aims and objectives a little faster, on top of saving communication costs.

To organize proper and productive meetings, consider the following guidelines:

✓ Ability to brainstorm for problem solving and decision-making

✓ Presentation skills and delegation abilities

✓ Basic understanding of motivation and personality

✓ Techniques of goal planning and project management

Holding a meeting can be expensive and time-consuming. Therefore, ensure to avoid wasting resources, money and time. For instance, instead of having to talk to your employees or co-workers in a face-to-face meeting, try video conferencing. Holding a virtual meeting through teleconferencing can also help you read facial expressions and body languages of the participants. If cost is not a problem, face-to-face meeting can help convey feelings and meaning albeit the expense of time.

These factors come at play when you are running or attending meetings:

✓ The aim of the meeting

✓ Your position and relationship with the participants

✓ Your role in the meeting, your confidence, experience, and personal aims, etc.

✓ The team, or the meeting delegates which depends on the needs and interests of the participants

✓ The situation and atmosphere, or background that prompted the meeting

✓ The organizational context which represents the needs and implications of the business or project or organization

Basic Rules of Holding Meetings

Once there is a need for a meeting, these rules can save time and make the meeting as productive as possible. These tips work best if you are the organizer of the meeting.

1. To plan, use the agenda as a planning tool

2. Ensure that you circulate the meeting agenda in advance

3. Try to run the meeting efficiently. For you to do that, you should keep your calm, and agree on the outcomes or actions. You should as well agree on the responsibilities and ensure to take notes.

4. Do not forget to write and circulate notes, particularly actions and accountabilities

5. Ensure to follow up agreed actions and delegated roles

How to Time Meetings

Timing meetings depends on the agenda of the meeting. As opposed to arbitrarily deciding the length of a meeting, try considering the time each item under discussion would take. For each of the agenda item, allocate an approximated time slot but keep the timings as realistic as possible.

The key here is having a precise time for each agenda and ensuring that the sessions run according to schedule. If you are running the meeting, avoid any circumstance that can bring failure. However, be aware that some items may consume longer times than allocated. Take control of the time and try to close various discussion topics in a bid to observe good timekeeping.

If you are planning for long meetings that involve participants from far, it is advisable to offer a pre-meeting 30 minutes prior to start time. Further, allocate a number of breaks to split long meetings that take 45-60 minutes. A 5-minutes break would do no harm and can allow your delegates to stretch their legs and breathe fresh air (which as we saw earlier, is an ideal way to refresh). Avoid the usual formal sit-down lunches at restaurants, as this usually lengthens lunch breaks by over 30 minutes.

Adopt working lunches, but begin with a 10-15 minutes for delegates to freshen off by moving outside the meeting room. In cases where delegates can only eat from restaurants, arrange a buffet and give them food choices earlier to save time.

Setting the Meeting Time

In most cases, meeting times often begin and end depending on the duration of the meeting and the availability of the participants. Holding a breakfast meeting can be a great idea, but can also be discomfort for some environments. Likewise, organizing a 2 hours meeting scheduled in the middle of the day can waste times in travel. In case the delegates are to travel from long distances, you can consider offering them overnight accommodation. Also, allocate enough time for delegates to travel home after the meeting, or ask them what they prefer in terms of their travel arrangements.

During Meetings: Time Saving Techniques

Mind Mapping

Mind mapping is the aspect of organizing ideas or notes into images for easier understanding. A mind map normally revolves around a single concept or idea represented as an image at the center of a blank page, from which associated ideas such as words or parts of words and images are added.

When drawing a mind map, you usually connect the major ideas to the central concept. The other ideas can then branch out from these. You can draw a mind map as a simple diagram, especially when in a hurry, such as during a lecture, or a complex image when you have the time.

If you are organizing a meeting, to save time when generating ideas, use mind maps. This technique is also a logical and creative means to take and make notes that literally map your ideas. Interestingly, all mind maps have one thing in common. They are organized in a structural manner that spreads out from the center, and they all use images, words, colors, symbols and lines in simple and brain friendly concepts.

The benefit of using mind mapping is that it converts a long and monotonous series of information into a memorable, colorful, and highly organized image that is compatible with your brain's natural way of functioning. One simple way you can understand the concept of mind mapping is to think of it as a city map.

The main idea is at the center just like a central business district in a major city. Then you have the main roads coming from the city center representing the key thoughts, the branches and subsidiary roads represent your secondary thoughts in a similar manner. Special shapes and images can represent particularly relevant ideas or landmarks of special interests.

Brainstorming

Brainstorming is best described as a spontaneous group discussion aimed at generating an idea or solution through a group discussion.Brainstorming has two phases: divergent thinking and convergent thinking. In the first phase, the divergent thinking phase, you, and the group generally come up with the topics and ideas you want to cover. During this stage, you let the ideas flow freely, not thinking about the good and bad stuff, or the semantically correct. At that time, there are no connections or relationships between your thoughts and all the ideas and thoughts are acceptable without judgment. You are thinking outside the box at this time and you are not restricted to any framework or set of rules.

In the second phase of brainstorming, the convergent thinking phase, there is a set of rules governing available options as you or other participants try to decide the best solution. Here, participants start organizing their thoughts, map them, and then work on finding a solution from the available tangibles.

At this stage, you deal with the created thoughts and ideas from the first stage, sieve the thoughts you perceive irrelevant and then organize the remaining information into finding a suitable solution. If used effectively, brainstorming can help you or other delegates save ample time and realize viable solutions for the company.

Note Taking

Even though you do not have to highlight every item under discussion, taking notes can help you record or remember details for future reference. The most recommendable tip to use when making notes is to be fully prepared. If you skip this step, you may end up losing plenty of information that you would have gained. To start, prepare a mind map with all the information you are already familiar with about the agenda or idea to be up for discussion.

Your mind works by linking new information to old existing information; which forms a framework that comprise of detailed information. Expand the mind map by incorporating new ideas for the business deal or idea addressed. When in a meeting session, it is always advisable to add new ideas to the agenda under discussion as you learn new and interesting information.

Minimize Meetings

Now and then, you may need to attend departmental meetings that may not be as important as the general or annual meetings. Regular meetings can sometimes become hideouts for employees who do not want to work. The best method is to invent a strategy that helps you avoid meeting unless they are unavoidable.

Working against the grain

Just because your colleagues do a certain task in a specific way does not mean that you have to do them the same way, if it is against your natural tendencies to work. If you can still get the work done without any errors and within the stipulated time, you can proceed to do it your way. Remember that your management is concerned about results obtained with accuracy and within the assigned time and not about how you do it, so long as it is not against the principles of your management. When you try to do something that you are not comfortable with, you end up wasting a lot of time.

These are some of the common mistakes that ought to be avoided when it comes to managing your time effectively.

Conclusion

I hope that you would have realized the importance of time management by the end of this eBook. Contrary to popular belief, time management is not rocket science. Conscious efforts from our end coupled with the determination to use our time productively will yield tremendous results.

Time is the most important asset that we have, not to forget a fast depleting one at that. This makes it all the more important for us to use this asset effectively before it is too late.

It is not possible to master the art of time management overnight. But with practice and grit, you will soon learn to manage your time and be surprised by how it has an impact on the various facets of your life.

I hope you found this book informative as well as inspiring. Thank you again for downloading this book!

Bonus

Thanks for making it this far in your education. If you want the real multiplier effect and to take your business skills to the next level, I recommend the easy-to-follow quick tips below. Whether you are running a company or just trying to free up some time so you can spend more time doing the things you love, get more done this week or your money back ;) (it's free!).

Go to https://funnelb.leadpages.co/smarter-not-harder-business/

Top 10 Productivity Tips & Hacks GUARANTEED to Unlock Massive Amounts of Time, Crush Decision Fatigue, and Skyrocket Your Efficiency and Effectiveness

Link: https://funnelb.leadpages.co/smarter-not-harder-business/

Recommended Reading

Complete Your Business Relationship Skills Education With a Click Away:

Management: Golden Nugget Methods to Manage Effectively - Teams, Personnel Management, Management Skills, and Conflict Resolution

Communication: Golden Nugget Methods to Communicate Effectively - Interpersonal, Influence, Social Skills, Listening

Take Your Business Skills Further for Financial Freedom or Corporate Dominance:

Small Business: EXACT BLUEPRINT on How to Start a Business - Home Business, Entrepreneur, and Small Business Marketing

Marketing: Golden Nuggets to Market Effectively - Internet Marketing, E-Commerce, Advertising & Web Marketing

<u>Sales: Foolproof Method to CRUSH Your Numbers -
Selling, Sales Techniques, and Sales Strategy</u>